GET THE F*CK UP

You're Not Done

The Art of
Reinventing Your Life

Brandon Meisner

Staten House

For Carolyn

Contents

VII

Prologue   XI

Part I - Acceptance   1

1. Accept Where You Are   3

Part II - Release   19

2. Let Go to Move Forward   21

3. Practice Self-Compassion   35

Part III - Rebuilding   51

4. Getting Clear on What You Want   53

5. Simplify Your Environment   69

6. Build Micro-Habits   85

7. Rebuild Your Confidence   101

Part IV - Redefinition   119

8. Redefine Your Identity   121

9. Embrace Uncertainty   137

10. Create New Routines & Rituals   153

Part V - Renewal   171

11. Surround Yourself with Growth Energy   173

12. Take Aligned Action   189

13. Find Meaning in the Mess   207

14. Design a Future That Feels Like You   223

Epilogue   241

"Every beginning holds a magic within it"

Hermann Hesse

Prologue

Embracing Change as a Constant

C hange has been a steady part of my life, something I have learned to expect rather than avoid. I've moved internationally four times, changed careers more times than I can count, and along the way, I've owned eleven homes and even a restaurant. Each chapter began with uncertainty — and a choice: to cling to the familiar or to trust the unknown. Every time, I chose to begin again.

At first, I thought reinvention meant starting over from scratch — new job, new address, new dream. But over time, I realized it's something deeper. Reinvention is about carrying forward the wisdom of where you've been while daring to rewrite what comes next. It's not about erasing your past, but expanding it — letting each version of yourself make room for the next.

At first, I believed that reinvention meant wiping the slate clean and starting over completely. I thought it involved a new job, a new home, and a fresh set of goals. However, over time, I realized reinvention is not just about getting rid of the past. It's a process that carries the lessons and experiences you have gathered and uses them to build something new. Think of it as renovating a house instead of demolishing it. You keep the foundation but change the rooms and decor to better suit your current needs.

For example, when I moved to a new city, I didn't leave behind everything about my previous life. I kept my values, my work ethic, and some of my hobbies. Instead, I adapted these to my new environment. This approach made reinvention feel less scary and more like a natural part of life. It's about adding layers to your story, letting each phase of your life inform the next one.

How Change Shapes Growth

Change often feels uncomfortable and disruptive. When you're faced with a big shift, like moving to a new place or starting a new career, it's easy to want to hold on tightly to what is familiar. But I have found that every change, even when it felt hard, made me stronger and more capable. For example, the first time I opened a business, I faced many mistakes and uncertainties. Those tough moments taught me problem-solving skills and resilience.

It helps to think of change not as an enemy but as a tool for growth. Stability is important, but without change, growth is impossible. Imagine a tree that never grows taller or spreads its branches in new directions. Change allows us to reach new heights and discover new parts of ourselves. Each new step, no matter how small, pushes you forward and helps you learn more about what you want and who you are.

Choosing to Reimagine Life

This story is not about running away from your current life or giving up on what you have built. Instead, it's about seeing your life in new ways and opening it to possibilities. You don't have to wait for a big event, like losing a job or moving, to start over. Starting over happens many times throughout life, as a cycle of endings and beginnings.

For example, you might decide to learn a new skill, change a daily habit, or reach out to new people. These small acts are forms of reinvention. Maybe you try cooking a new type of cuisine or sign up for a class that interests you. These steps may seem simple, but they can lead to meaningful changes over time. This ongoing process lets you shape your life according to what feels right at different moments.

Inviting Yourself to Keep Growing

When you look at your life as a work in progress, it becomes easier to accept that you are not finished yet. You don't have to have everything figured out or stick to one version of yourself. Every decision to change, no matter how small, is a sign that you're continuing to grow.

You have likely already experienced many forms of reinvention. Maybe you've changed your routine, taken a new job, or overcome a difficult situation. Now, it can be helpful to do this with intention. This means deciding with purpose how you want to move forward and what kind of life you want to create. For example, you might set a goal to improve your health, learn a language, or dedicate more time to hobbies.

Each new day, each decision to try again, is an opportunity to shape your story. It's proof that it's never too late to start fresh or make changes that reflect who you are now. This is the essence of living a life that evolves and grows, that welcomes new experiences, and that stays open to the possibilities ahead.

Delete that old version of yourself you have in your head - it's expired!

Part I
Acceptance
Facing Reality

Chapter 1

Accept Where You Are

E very fresh start begins with a simple but difficult truth: you can't move forward until you stop fighting where you are.

So many of us try to start over by running — from regret, from loss, from failure, from the versions of ourselves we wish we could erase. But real change doesn't come from escape; it begins with acceptance.

Acceptance isn't resignation. It's not giving up or saying, *"This is as good as it gets"* or *"It is what it is."*

Acceptance is honesty. It's the courage to look at your life — the beautiful, the broken, and the in-between — and say, *"This is my reality right now, and I can build from here."*

No transformation can happen without that first act of truth-telling. Before you rewrite your story, you have to acknowledge the page you're on.

Stop Fighting Reality

Understanding Resistance to Reality

It is common for people to struggle with what life has given them. When things don't go as expected or hoped for, it's natural to feel frustrated or disappointed. Many find themselves wishing things had been different, thinking about decisions made in the past, and holding on to ideas about what should have been. This kind of thinking takes up a lot of energy. You might find yourself replaying moments in your head or even blaming yourself or others. But focusing so much on the past or on how unfair life seems doesn't help create a better future. Instead, it can make you feel stuck and powerless.

Why Fighting Reality Drains You

When you spend your time and energy resisting reality, you are fighting against something that you cannot change. Imagine trying to push a big rock up a hill – it takes a lot of effort, and you might not make any progress. This effort uses up your strength and attention, which might be better spent on taking steps forward. For example, if you lost a job, getting angry or upset won't give you a new one. Instead, if you accept the situation, you can focus on updating your resume, reaching out to contacts, or learning new skills. This practical action can lead to change and new opportunities.

What Acceptance Really Means

Acceptance doesn't mean you have to like or agree with what has happened. It's not about pretending everything is perfect or ignoring your feelings. Rather, acceptance means you stop arguing with what is real. It means that instead of saying, "*This shouldn't be happening,*" you say, "*Okay, this is happening, what can I do about it now?*" Think of acceptance as looking at a map before you start a journey. You might not like the path you see, but knowing the path helps you decide where to go next.

Moving from Resistance to Action

When you let go of resisting reality, you free up energy you can use to build something new. This shift changes your focus from what is wrong to what you can do next. For example, if you have finished school but can't find a job in your field, instead of only feeling upset, acceptance might lead you to explore other kinds of work, internships, or further training. Every step you take moves you forward. The key is to think about what you can change rather than what you can't.

Turning Energy Toward Rebuilding

Every moment you stop fighting the facts, you reclaim your power. You regain control over your actions and choices. This is important because feeling powerless can make problems seem even bigger. When you choose acceptance, you acknowledge your reality but also your ability to take steps to improve it. You can then use your energy as fuel to rebuild your life in a way that suits you. For example, after a breakup, you might feel sad, but acceptance helps you focus on activities that make you happy, reconnecting with friends, or even exploring new interests.

Acceptance as a Source of Strength

Some people think accepting a tough situation is a sign of giving up or weakness. However, acceptance is actually one of the strongest things you can do. It shows that you are facing reality clearly and honestly. This grounded awareness is the base on which change is built. Take a mountain climber as an example. Before climbing, they carefully study the mountain and prepare. Acceptance of the challenges ahead helps them plan properly rather than rushing in blindly. Similarly, accepting your current situation allows you to plan your next actions wisely.

Acceptance Lays the Groundwork for New Beginnings

Sometimes we want a fresh start but don't know how to make it happen. Acceptance is the foundation for every real new beginning. Without accepting where you are now, it's hard to move forward. Imagine trying to build a house on shaky ground. No matter how good the plans are, the house won't stand. But when the ground is stable, you can create something strong and lasting. Acceptance stabilizes your inner world so you can build the life you want step by step.

Practical Steps to Practice Acceptance

Acknowledge your feelings. It's okay to feel upset about things that have happened. Write down your thoughts or talk to someone you trust to get your emotions out.

Stop arguing with reality. When you catch yourself saying, "This shouldn't be happening," gently remind yourself, "It is happening. What can I do next?"

Focus on the present. Instead of dwelling on the past, try to bring your attention to what you can do today or this week.

Set small goals. Break down your situation into manageable pieces. For example, if looking for a job feels overwhelming, aim to look at three job postings a day.

Take action based on your acceptance. Use the energy from letting go of resistance to make concrete moves, like updating a resume, signing up for a course, or reaching out to a support group.

Acceptance is not about giving up or liking how things are. It's about stopping the mental fight and starting to use your energy to create something better. When you let go of resisting what is, you free yourself to shape what will be.

Acknowledge Mistakes Without Self-Hate

Facing the Choices That Led You Here

Starting over is never easy. One of the hardest parts is admitting to yourself the choices that brought you to this point. Maybe you trusted someone who wasn't trustworthy. For example, you might have shared your deepest secrets or relied on their advice, only to be let down. Sometimes, people stay in situations longer than they should, hoping things will get better, but they just don't. You might have ignored your gut feeling or signs that something was wrong, convincing yourself that everything was fine. It's also possible that you've failed in ways you never expected, like not reaching a goal or making a bad decision that hurt you or others. These are all human experiences, and facing them can feel painful.

The Importance of Acknowledging Mistakes with Kindness

Admitting that you made mistakes is an important step toward healing. But it matters how you do this. When you recognize your errors, it helps to do so with kindness, not with harsh self-criticism. Imagine if a friend told you they made a mistake; you would likely respond with understanding and support. You deserve to treat yourself the same way. Being mean to yourself only makes it harder to move on. Compassion allows you to see mistakes as part of being human instead of proof that you're a bad person. For example, writing down what you learned from a mistake or talking kindly to yourself in the mirror can build that compassion.

Understanding How Self-Hate Holds You Back

Self-hate is a powerful barrier that keeps you stuck in the past. It tells you lies like, "Because you made that mistake, you are a mistake." This isn't true. It's your shame speaking, not your real self. Shame is an intense feeling that makes you want to hide or avoid others. It creates a mental loop where you keep blaming yourself without trying to fix the problem or grow. For instance, if someone fails at a job interview, self-hate might make them believe they will never succeed at anything. The truth is, mistakes do not define who you are; they are just moments in your life, not the whole story.

You Are More Than Your Failures

You are not simply the collection of your failures. Instead, you are the person who learns from those failures and tries again. Learning from mistakes means looking at what happened and asking honest questions like, "*What can I do differently next time?*" or "*What did this teach me about myself?*" It takes courage to face your own faults without running away. This bravery is something to respect and appreciate in yourself. For example, if you once trusted the wrong people, learning to set healthy boundaries next time is valuable growth. Recognizing your growth can motivate you to keep moving forward, even when it feels hard.

Separating Actions from Identity

Moving forward is easier when you separate what you did from who you are. You might have made decisions or taken actions that you regret, but these actions do not make up your entire identity. Think of your actions as chapters in your life story, not the whole book. For example, if someone made a mistake at work or in a relationship, it doesn't mean they are a bad person overall. It means they made a choice in a specific moment that can be learned from. Understanding this separation helps you avoid labeling yourself negatively and instead focus on growth and change.

Finding Redemption in Compassion

No matter what happened, you are not beyond redemption. Redemption means finding a way back to a good place after being lost in a bad one. Every mistake can become a lesson if you treat yourself with compassion instead of contempt. Contempt is when you look down on yourself and hold feelings of disgust or anger toward yourself. Compassion is the opposite — it means treating yourself as you would a good friend who is struggling. For instance, if you made a decision that hurt someone, compassion might involve apologizing, making amends, and promising yourself to do better. This process allows healing and new growth.

Forgiving Yourself to Move On

Forgiving yourself does not mean excusing what happened in the past. It doesn't mean pretending the mistakes didn't matter. Instead, forgiving yourself means choosing not to live frozen in those old moments. It means deciding that your past won't control your future. Forgiveness is a form of freedom. It lets you stop feeling burdened by guilt and shame. For example, you might say, "I regret what happened, but I choose to learn and move on." This choice makes room for new experiences, happiness, and success. When you forgive yourself, you open the door to a fresh start.

This Is Your Current Chapter, Not Your Ending

Understanding Difficult Seasons as Part of a Larger Story

It's common to think that when life gets really hard, it means you've reached a stopping point, a dead end. However, the hard time you are going through right now is not where your story finishes. Instead, it is just one part of a bigger story. Think of your life as a book. Every chapter tells part of your story, but no single chapter shows everything. The struggles and challenges you face are one chapter, not the whole book. This idea helps remind us that difficult moments don't last forever or define everything about us. They are just moments in time.

Right now, you may feel a mix of feelings like loss, confusion, or sadness. This time might seem quiet or slow, like things are not moving forward. You might be figuring out what to do next or what direction to take. This stage is like rebuilding after something falls apart. It can be hard to see progress because it often happens slowly and in small steps. Remember that this time is necessary and important in your growth.

You Are Still Becoming and Growing

One important thing to know is that you are still becoming the person you want to be. Growing and changing happens little by little. It is not something that stops suddenly. Everyone is in the middle of growing their whole life, learning new things and trying to improve. Being in a tough spot doesn't stop this process. In fact, it might even help you learn new lessons or find new strength.

It is also okay to keep dreaming. Sometimes when things are hard, people stop hoping or dreaming about good things because they feel too far away or impossible. But dreams are part of what helps us keep moving forward. You can allow yourself to think about what you want for your future, no matter what is happening right now. This is a way to keep hope alive.

Trying again is also part of growing. If something didn't work out, that does not mean you are done. You have the chance to start over, take new steps, and build something new. The things you create after hard times can be very meaningful. For example, if you lost a job, trying again might mean looking for new opportunities or learning new skills. This effort to rebuild shows your courage and resilience.

When Endings Feel Like the Only Thing

Sometimes, when everything you are used to changes or falls apart, it feels like you are at the end of the road. This can be very painful because the familiarity is gone. You might feel lost or unsure about what to do next. It is natural to feel this way when something important ends.

But endings are not always final. They can also be places where new beginnings start. It is like how the end of one day is the start of a new one. You might not realize yet that this ending is actually making room for something new to grow. For example, if you end a friendship or a relationship, it can feel very final at first. However, after some time, you might find new friends or develop new connections that bring happiness.

Seeing this requires patience and time. The new beginning might be hidden or unclear right now, but it is there. Recognizing that your story still has more chapters can help you feel less stuck.

Holding On Through the Hard Parts

It can be tempting to want to escape or rush through this difficult time. The pain and discomfort make us want to get to the next part quickly. But going through these feelings is important. Holding on means staying present with what is happening, even if it feels uncomfortable.

For example, if you are grieving, allow yourself to feel the sadness without trying to ignore it or pretend it's not there. If you lost a job, don't rush into another without taking time to think about what you want next. Living through the experience fully, with all its ups and downs, helps you grow stronger and wiser.

When you hold on through hard moments, you start to see that what seems like breaking down is actually part of becoming stronger and better equipped for what is ahead. It is like how a seed in the ground looks like it is dying, but it is really growing roots before it breaks through the soil.

Taking Your Time with This Chapter of Your Life

This chapter of your life is important and deserves your full attention. It is easy to want to close it fast and move on, but that can make you miss important lessons. Take the time to live this experience. Notice what you learn about yourself, about others, and about life in general.

Lessons from hard times often teach patience, kindness, and strength. For example, you might learn how to ask for help or how to set new boundaries. Maybe you learn what really matters to you or what kind of person you want to become. These lessons will help you in future chapters.

Let this chapter shape you. Allow it to influence how you think, how you act, and how you feel. This shaping will prepare you for the next parts of your story. Even if you can't see what comes next right now, the growth happening in this time will help you handle what the future brings.

Living through this chapter means noticing the small changes and improvements too. For instance, maybe you start a new hobby, or you meet a new person who brings positive energy. These small things are part of your story's growth and healing.

By not rushing, you give yourself the chance to build a solid foundation for what comes next. When you finally turn the page to a new chapter, you will be stronger and more ready because of everything you went through before.

Closing Reflection

Accepting where you are is not the final step — it's the first.
It's the act of standing still long enough to see clearly. It's the moment you decide that even though you can't change the past, you can choose what comes next.

Stop fighting reality — it's already here.
Acknowledge your mistakes — they're proof that you've lived and learned.
And remind yourself: this is not your ending. It's the doorway to a new beginning.

The moment you accept where you are, you reclaim your power to move forward — not as who you were, but as who you're becoming.

Part II
Release

Letting Go of the Past

Chapter 2

Let Go to Move Forward

S tarting over is not just about what you begin — it's about what you release.

We can't step into a new life while dragging the weight of the old one behind us. The past has a way of clinging to us: in memories, objects, regrets, and old wounds we keep reopening. Letting go doesn't mean forgetting what happened; it means freeing yourself from the power it holds over you.

To move forward, you must loosen your grip on what no longer serves you.

You can't reach for the next chapter if both hands are clenched around yesterday.

Let Go of Grudges and Regrets

The Harm of Holding on to Resentment

Holding on to resentment can be very painful. Imagine you are holding something hot, like a burning coal. It hurts your hand the whole time you hold it. Resentment works the same way. When you keep feeling angry or upset about something that happened, you are hurting yourself over and over again. The person or situation you are upset about might not even feel your pain. You are the one who keeps feeling bad because you won't let go.

Resentment is like a heavy weight that makes it hard to move forward. It can affect your mood, health, and your ability to enjoy life. People who carry a lot of resentment might feel stressed, restless, or even have trouble sleeping. This is why it is important to find ways to let go of resentment so you can feel better and live more peacefully.

How Grudges and Regrets Grow Stronger

Grudges and regrets don't usually go away on their own. In fact, they often get stronger the more you think about them. When you keep replaying bad memories in your mind, you are making them bigger and harder to forget. This is because your brain remembers those feelings of pain or anger every time you think about the past.

For example, if someone betrayed your trust, you might find yourself going over the exact moment it happened. You might replay the conversation or details repeatedly, hoping to find a way to fix it or understand why it happened. But thinking about it all the time does not give you control over the situation. Instead, it keeps the hurt alive.

What It Means to Let Go of Grudges

Letting go of grudges does not mean you have to say what happened was okay. It doesn't mean you must forget the wrongs or that they didn't matter. It simply means you choose not to let those feelings take over your life. You stop letting those bad memories poison your thoughts and feelings every day.

For example, if a friend hurt you, letting go means you might still feel sadness or anger about what happened. But you decide not to carry those negative feelings around all the time. This does not mean you have to be best friends with that person again or trust them fully. It just means you are not holding on to the pain anymore so you can be free to enjoy your present.

Understanding Regret and Responsibility

Regret is a feeling many people know well. It is often mixed with the idea of responsibility. Sometimes, we think that if we punish ourselves for past mistakes, it means we are taking responsibility. But true responsibility is different from self-punishment.

True responsibility means being aware of what went wrong, learning from it, and using that knowledge to do better next time. For example, if you made a mistake at work, feeling guilty all the time will not fix the mistake. Instead, understanding why it happened and taking steps to improve will help you grow and avoid making the same mistake again.

A Simple Technique to Let Go of Painful Memories

When you feel hurt or upset by a memory, you can try a simple technique to help you let go. When the memory comes up, stop for a moment. Take a deep breath and say to yourself, "*That happened. I can't change it, but I can change how I carry it.*"

This sentence helps remind you that the past cannot be changed, but you have control over how it affects you now. You don't need to forget what happened or pretend it was nothing. You just don't want to feed that memory with more anger or sadness.

Releasing Old Stories to Find Peace

Every time you stop yourself from replaying a painful story, you gain a little more peace. It feels like putting down a heavy bag you have been carrying. You give yourself permission to live without being trapped by the past.

For example, if you used to think about a time someone hurt your feelings every day, trying this technique might help you think about it less often. Each time you choose not to focus on the pain, you make room for happier thoughts. Over time, this can help you feel lighter and more free from the pain of that memory.

Being Patient with Yourself

Letting go of resentment and regret is not easy, and it does not happen overnight. It often takes time and effort. Sometimes, you might find yourself caught in the same thoughts again. This is normal. When it happens, use the technique again and be kind to yourself.

You can also try writing down your feelings. Putting your thoughts on paper can help you understand them better and see things more clearly. Talking with a friend or a counselor can also give you support and new ideas on how to move forward.

Taking Care of Your Present

When you let go of grudges and regrets, you make space for taking care of your present life. You can focus more on the things and people that bring you joy. Activities like exercising, spending time with loved ones, or enjoying hobbies can help you feel better.

For example, instead of replaying a painful memory, you could go for a walk, listen to music, or work on something you enjoy. These actions help your mind focus on positive things and improve your mood.

Growing Through Self-Awareness

The key to moving on from resentment and regret is self-awareness. This means paying attention to your feelings without judgment. Notice when you start to feel angry or sad about the past. Recognize what you are thinking and feeling.

Then, choose to respond differently. Instead of letting the past control you, decide to grow from the experience. Use what you have learned to make better choices in the future.

This might mean saying no to situations that harm you, setting boundaries with people, or trying new ways to solve problems. Each step you take shows that you are responsible for your own life and happiness.

Remove Reminders That Trigger Old Pain

The Past Hides in Plain Sight

The past is often with us in ways we might not immediately notice. It lives in the photos that stay stuck in the same place on our walls or in our devices. These photos can be from moments we want to remember, but sometimes, they freeze a memory that hurts instead of helps. The messages on our phones or computers that we never delete can also hold us back. Even if these old messages remind us of good times, they sometimes bring pain when we read them again. Then there are the objects we keep. Maybe it is a gift from someone who was once important, or a thing that used to represent hope and dreams. But when looking at these objects causes sadness, they become like invisible chains holding us to a past we want to move beyond.

Detaching from the Past by Changing Your Physical Space

One way to begin moving on is to make changes in the spaces where you live and spend time. For example, if you have a gift from a relationship that has ended, you might consider donating it. Giving it away can be a way to let go of the memories attached to that gift. Another action could be deleting old conversations on your phone or social media. These chats can sometimes reopen wounds when you accidentally reread them. Clearing them out helps stop re-living those painful moments over and over. You can also rearrange your living space. Changing where furniture is placed, getting new decorations, or adding things that remind you of who you are now can help. This means making your home reflect your current life and not the life you lost.

The Power of Clearing Space in Your Life

Clearing space isn't just about cleaning your home—it's about creating room in your heart and mind too. When you take away things that belong to your old story, you create space for new experiences and feelings. For example, if you remove old letters or photos that make you sad, you allow yourself to notice new moments that bring happiness. It's like opening a window in a stuffy room so fresh air can come in. The act of clearing space shows you are ready for change, even if it feels scary. This new space can help you invite new friends, new ideas, and new emotions into your life.

Starting Small to Let Go

You don't have to let go of everything all at once. It can feel overwhelming to try to erase all memories or objects connected to your past. Instead, choose one small thing to begin with. It might be a single photograph, a small object, or even a habit like scrolling through old messages every day. Decide to release that one thing. This simple act can feel powerful because it is a choice you make consciously. When you decide to let go, try to do it with kindness toward yourself. You can even say a small phrase or whisper to it: "*Thank you for what you taught me. I don't need you anymore.*" This helps you close that chapter with respect for your past, without letting it keep controlling you.

Healing as Reclamation, Not Erasure

Healing isn't about erasing your past or pretending it never happened. It's about taking back control of your life story. You are not the sum of your old memories or the pain you have felt. You are the person who chooses which parts of your past you keep and which parts you leave behind. For example, you might keep lessons learned from past relationships but choose to move on from the hurt those relationships caused. This process of choosing means you honor your growth and your strength. It's about building a life where you decide what matters and what no longer serves you. Through this, you reclaim your own power and create space for a future full of new possibilities.

Forgive Yourself So You Can Move Forward

Understanding the Challenge of Self-Forgiveness

One of the hardest people to forgive is often the person we see in the mirror every day — ourselves. When we think about mistakes we've made or moments we regret, it's easy to get stuck replaying those times over and over in our minds. These can be the things we said and wish we hadn't, or the things we didn't say but wish we had. Sometimes, they are moments when we feel we should have acted differently or known better. This constant replay creates a heavy burden, making it difficult to let go and move forward.

Self-forgiveness doesn't mean ignoring what happened or pretending everything was okay. It is not a kind of weakness or denial. Instead, self-forgiveness is about showing yourself kindness and understanding. It means looking honestly at what happened without being overly harsh or judgmental. When you forgive yourself, you choose to stop repeating negative thoughts that condemn you and instead start thinking in a way that helps you heal.

Recognizing Your Effort and Growth

The first step in forgiving yourself is to recognize that at the time, you did the best you could with what you knew. Nobody has perfect knowledge or perfect judgment at every moment. Everyone makes mistakes, and that's part of being human. It helps to remind yourself that your choices weren't perfect, but that doesn't mean you are a bad person. Hating or blaming yourself over and over will not change what happened, but it will keep you stuck in sadness and pain.

Try this simple practice: say to yourself, "*I was learning. I was growing. I can forgive who I was because I am still becoming.*" Saying these words out loud can help your mind and heart accept that you are not the same person you were in the past. You are always changing and learning from your experiences.

Moving Past Self-Blame

When you hold on to self-blame, it can feel like you are living among ruins — broken pieces of mistakes and regrets. It's important to realize that you cannot build a new life or new happiness while you are standing in those ruins. You need to take a step away from blaming yourself to make room for healing and peace. This means choosing to stop punishing yourself for being human.

The process of letting go might take time. Sometimes, you may feel guilt or shame creeping back in. When that happens, try to gently remind yourself that everyone slips up, and that doesn't mean you are less worthy of kindness and happiness. You can also try writing down your thoughts or talking to a trusted friend or counselor who can help you see things more clearly.

Using Forgiveness as a Bridge to the Future

Think of forgiveness as a bridge — something that connects your past with the life you want to create going forward. Forgiving yourself does not erase what happened, but it helps you take control of your story. It allows you to learn from your past without being trapped by it.

A helpful way to start is by identifying at least one small thing you can do today to be kind to yourself. This could be taking a walk, writing a positive note, or simply saying, "*I am allowed to make mistakes.*" Building these small habits can help you feel stronger and more hopeful over time.

By choosing forgiveness, you open the door to your potential. You give yourself permission to heal, grow, and move toward a better future. The bridge may feel shaky at first, but every step you take makes it stronger and clearer.

Closing Reflection

Letting go is not an event — it's a practice. Some days, the past will whisper to you, asking to be remembered, replayed, relived. When it does, gently remind yourself: *I choose peace over pain. I choose freedom over familiarity.*

You are not what happened to you.
You are not the person who made those mistakes.
You are the person who decided to start again.

And that decision — that single, quiet act of release — is where your new life begins.

Chapter 3

Practice Self-Compassion

.

.

B eginning again isn't just about changing your life — it's about
changing the way you treat yourself along the way.
When you've lost your way or are trying to rebuild, self-compassion isn't
a luxury. It's the foundation that makes growth sustainable.

Many of us are kind to others but cruel to ourselves. We tell friends, *"It's
okay, you're doing your best,"* but tell ourselves, *"You should have known
better."*

We offer comfort to others and criticism to ourselves. But you cannot
heal through hostility — not even when it's your own voice doing the
fighting.

To start again, you must learn the art of gentleness and rest. Not
indulgence, not avoidance — but kindness with courage.

Speak to Yourself the Way You'd Speak to a Friend

Seeing Yourself Through a Friend's Eyes

Imagine your closest friend sitting right in front of you, their eyes full of tears and their voice shaky as they tell you about the fears and doubts they carry inside. They might talk about feeling like a failure or regretting the choices they have made. Now, think about how you would respond to them in that moment. You wouldn't criticize or shout. You wouldn't list everything they had done wrong or call them weak. Instead, you would listen carefully. You'd let them know they are human, and that it's okay to feel this way sometimes. You would tell them their story isn't finished yet, and that there is still hope for better days ahead.

The question to ask yourself is: why shouldn't you treat yourself with the same kindness? Why do we often talk to ourselves in ways we would never use with someone we care about? This is the place where understanding self-compassion becomes important. Treating yourself like a friend means offering patience and understanding when things go wrong, not harsh judgment.

Understanding the Voices in Your Head

Most people hear voices inside their head that judge and criticize instead of guide and support. These voices might say things like "You're not good enough," or "You've messed up again." Often, we confuse these harsh inner messages with being responsible or motivated. We believe that if we don't push ourselves hard enough using shame or fear, we won't improve. But this is not true. It's important to recognize that cruelty inside your mind won't help you grow. Real growth comes from being warm and kind to yourself, even when things are tough.

To change this habit of harsh self-talk, you can start by paying attention to your inner conversations. Notice when your thoughts turn negative or mean. These moments are chances to practice kindness by gently correcting those thoughts and speaking to yourself in a caring way.

Changing Your Inner Dialogue: Simple Steps to Practice

Changing how you talk to yourself takes time and practice. One way to do this is by catching your negative thoughts and then deliberately turning them into something more positive and true. For example, if you catch yourself thinking, "I've ruined everything," stop and say instead, "I've made mistakes, but I can learn from them." This small change matters because it shifts your mind away from blame and towards learning.

Another common thought might be, "I'm not doing enough." When you notice this, try saying, "I'm doing my best for where I am right now." This kind of self-talk acknowledges your efforts and gives you credit for trying, even if things aren't perfect. It's okay to recognize that you are working hard, even if you have more to do later.

To practice this, you can write down some of the negative thoughts that often come up for you. Then, next to each one, write a kinder or more realistic way to say it. Keep this list somewhere you can see it often, like on your desk or your phone. It can help remind you to speak gently to yourself when you need it most.

Your Mind Is Like a Home

Think about your thoughts as the environment you live in, like the home you come back to every day. If your mind is filled with harsh, critical voices, it's like living in a house where the windows are always closed, and it feels hard to breathe. When your mind is a safe and supportive place, it's like having fresh air and sunshine. You feel more comfortable and free to be yourself.

You don't need to be your own biggest critic to improve or get better at something. People often believe that pushing themselves hard with negative talk will make them work harder. But actually, when you are kind to yourself, you build strength from a more solid and healthy place. Being your own ally means standing by yourself with kindness, just like a good friend would—supporting you while still encouraging you to do your best.

Balancing Kindness and Strength

Being kind to yourself doesn't mean ignoring problems or pretending everything is perfect. It's about being firm but fair. Picture how you would advise a good friend who is struggling—sometimes you encourage them firmly to keep going, but always gently. You can do this for yourself as well. For example, if you find it hard to keep to a task or goal, you might say, "I'm not there yet, but I will keep trying," instead of, "I'm a failure." This gives you a chance to grow without beating yourself up.

Try to notice when you are too hard on yourself and pause. Ask if you would say those words to a friend. If the answer is no, it's a good signal to change your self-talk. Replace harsh thoughts with words that support and encourage you.

Practical Ways to Build Self-Compassion Daily

To make this kind of self-talk a habit, try setting aside some time each day to check in with yourself. You might spend a few minutes writing in a journal or just sitting quietly and noticing your thoughts. When negative thoughts come up, pause and gently shift them. For example, you might say, "I am okay, even though this is hard." Over time, these moments add up and change the way you feel inside.

Another way to build kindness toward yourself is to do little things you enjoy and that make you feel good. This might be going for a walk, reading a favorite book, or cooking a meal you like. These acts are ways to show yourself care in a physical way, supporting the kindness you want to have inside.

It also helps to remind yourself that everyone struggles sometimes. You're not alone in having fears, regrets, or doubts. Knowing that other people have these feelings too can make it easier to be gentle with yourself.

You Can't Shame Yourself Into Change

For a long time, many people thought that feeling guilty or ashamed would help them stay on track and grow as individuals. They believed guilt kept them disciplined and shame made them humble. But this isn't true. Shame doesn't help you change for the better; instead, it stops you from moving forward. When you shame yourself, you don't grow. You just get stuck. Change doesn't come from beating yourself down. It comes from starting to care about yourself and wanting to be whole again.

Shame feels like trying to run forward while looking backward. Imagine trying to walk while only watching your feet or the ground behind you. You'll probably trip and fall because you're not paying attention to what's in front of you. This is what happens when you focus too much on your past mistakes or things you did wrong. You get stuck in those moments and forget about the future. When you keep reminding yourself of your faults, your brain starts to think that growing means feeling pain and discomfort. So, it's no surprise that moving forward feels so hard.

What we all need to understand is that change happens when you feel safe. If you live in fear of punishment or harsh judgment, growing becomes scary. But when you feel safe inside yourself, change becomes easier. Feeling safe means knowing your mistakes won't bring cruelty or harshness from you or others. It means trusting that you can take chances without being rejected or feeling unworthy. This safe feeling lets you try again after a failure and keep growing without fear.

True accountability sounds very different from self-shaming. When someone holds themselves accountable, they don't say, "I'm worthless." Instead, they say, "I could have done better, and I will next time." This small change in how you talk to yourself matters a lot. The first way, filled with shame, destroys your confidence and stops you from trying again. The second way, based on love and hope, helps you rebuild yourself and move forward stronger.

Another important thing is to stop thinking that you need to suffer to get better. This idea is common but wrong. You don't have to punish yourself to make progress. Forgiving yourself is not something you have to earn; it's something you simply need to accept. Instead of waiting to feel worthy or forgiven, start showing up for yourself in a new way today. Treat yourself with kindness and patience. This new approach encourages growth, healing, and change much more than harsh self-criticism ever will.

Rest Is Part of Rebuilding, Not a Reward for It

When you are starting over in life, it feels like you have to keep doing something all the time. You might think that if you keep moving or working, you can fix everything faster. It is easy to believe that doing more will solve your problems. But rebuilding your life does not only happen when you are busy or active. It also happens when you are still and resting. Rest is not just a break you get after you have done something important. It is actually a time to remember your own value, your worth.

Why Rest Is Important for Your Energy and Mind

When you are tired and empty inside, you cannot put energy into rebuilding your life. Trying to move forward when you have no strength leaves you feeling empty. It is like pouring water from an empty cup. You cannot keep giving to yourself or others if you have nothing left inside. Also, if you are burned out, you cannot think clearly. When your mind and body are worn out because you spent so much time trying to escape pain, it becomes hard to see what to do next. Rest gives you a chance to refill your energy. When you allow yourself to stop and recharge, you give your brain a break to recover and become sharp again.

Rest Is Not Laziness, It Is Repair

Sometimes people think that resting is lazy or avoiding work. But resting is the opposite of laziness. It is an important part of fixing yourself. When you sleep, your body works on healing any damage, even if you don't feel it. Your body takes that time to rebuild cells and regain strength. The same idea applies to your emotions. When you let yourself rest emotionally, your heart can heal from the hurt it felt. Emotional rest might mean not thinking about problems for a little while or doing something that makes you feel calm. Both physical and emotional rest help you fix parts of yourself that got broken during hard times.

How to Give Yourself Permission to Rest

Many people feel like resting is a waste of time or that they need to keep pushing forward without stopping. But it is important to give yourself permission to pause and take breaks. For example, you could spend a whole day doing nothing at all. You don't have to rush to fix everything on that day. Or, you could take a walk without any goal in mind. Just walking without trying to get somewhere is a way to let your mind rest. Another example is sitting quietly by yourself without planning the next step in your life. All of these simple actions are not wasting time. Instead, they restore the strength you will need for the challenges you will face later.

How Rest Helps You Keep Going

Starting over is hard work. It can feel overwhelming and sometimes you might want to give up, especially if you do not feel strong enough. Rest helps you avoid reaching that breaking point. When you take time to rest, you protect yourself from burning out or feeling hopeless in the middle of your journey. Rest gives your body a chance to heal and your mind a chance to clear away confusion. Without rest, it is easy to lose hope and stop trying. But when you rest, you keep the energy and desire to continue moving forward, even when things are difficult.

Practical Ways to Rest While Rebuilding

If you are rebuilding your life, you might not be sure how to rest in a way that helps. One practical way is to create a rest routine. This could include going to bed at the same time every night to get enough sleep. You can also try breathing exercises to calm your mind when you feel overwhelmed. Another helpful step is to take regular breaks during your day. For instance, after working for an hour, take five or ten minutes to step away and do nothing related to your work or stress. You could also plan short activities that make you feel good but do not require much effort, like listening to soft music or sitting outside enjoying nature. Small steps like these restore energy and make rebuilding easier.

Emotional Rest and Its Role in Healing

Rest is not just about the body; your emotions need rest too. Emotional rest means giving yourself time to feel your feelings without trying to fix them immediately. For example, if you feel sad, allow yourself to sit with that sadness for a while, instead of pushing it away. Writing down your thoughts in a journal can be a form of emotional rest. It helps you process your feelings and understand them better. Talking to a trusted friend or counselor without trying to solve problems right away can also provide emotional rest. This kind of rest helps your heart and mind heal the pain and prepares you for the work of rebuilding.

Rest as Part of Your Daily Life

Rest should not be something you do only after everything else is done. Instead, it should be a regular part of your daily routine. When you start to think rest is only for after you have "earned" it, you might never allow yourself to stop. Think of rest as a necessary step to keep going, not as an extra reward. Building rest into your daily life can be simple. You can set reminders to take deep breaths during the day. Quiet moments, even a few minutes long, can help you feel more grounded. Doing gentle stretches or meditation before bed can help your body relax. These small daily habits of rest prepare you for the bigger work of changing your life.

Understanding Rest as a Support, Not a Hindrance

It is easy to believe resting slows you down or stops you from reaching your goals. But rest actually supports your progress. Without rest, your body and mind get tired and stop working well. When you build in rest, you keep your energy steady. You also keep your mind clear, helping you make better decisions. Rest helps you see your situation more clearly instead of getting lost in stress or frustration. When you feel stronger and more focused, your actions become more effective. Taking breaks and resting is not stopping; it is getting ready to move forward with power.

Building a Healthy Relationship With Rest

Sometimes people feel guilty about resting because they think they should always be busy. To build a healthy relationship with rest, it is important to change that mindset. Think of rest as part of self-care, just like eating healthy food or exercising. Rest helps your whole body and mind work better. You can practice telling yourself that resting does not mean you are weak. It means you are wise enough to take care of yourself. Start small, by adding a few minutes of rest to your day. Notice how your body and mind feel afterward. With time, you will see that rest is a strong tool in rebuilding your life.

What Happens When You Ignore Rest

Ignoring rest can lead to many problems. Without rest, your body might become sick or hurt more easily. You may feel tired all the time and have trouble concentrating. Emotionally, you might feel overwhelmed, anxious, or even depressed. When you try to keep going without breaks, your progress slows down. You might make poor decisions because your mind is tired. Rest is not a weakness, but a prevention tool. By resting, you avoid hitting a point where your body and mind break down. Taking time to rest prevents these problems and keeps your rebuilding process on track.

Closing Reflection

Self-compassion is not the soft alternative to discipline — it *is* the discipline. It's the practice of showing up for yourself again and again with gentleness, even when you feel undeserving.

So, as you rebuild your life:

Speak kindly to yourself, especially when it's hardest.

Reject shame as a path to growth — it never leads anywhere worth going.

Rest without guilt, knowing that healing happens in both movement and stillness.

The most powerful transformation doesn't come from force. It comes from acceptance, care, and patience — from treating yourself like someone worth saving, because you are.

Every time you choose compassion over criticism, you lay another stone in the foundation of your new life.
And one day, you'll look around and realize — you didn't just start over. You began again with love.

Part III
Rebuilding
Creating Structure & Confidence

.

Chapter 4

Getting Clear on What You Want

B eginning again can feel like standing at the edge of a vast, empty field. The possibilities are endless — and that can be both exhilarating and paralyzing. When you're trying to rebuild your life, clarity is your compass. Without it, you drift, guided by habits, other people's expectations, or leftover regrets.

Getting clear on what you want isn't about knowing every detail of your future. It's about knowing the direction that feels true to you, right now. It's about deciding which life you're willing to work for and what you're unwilling to compromise.

Define the Kind of Life You'd Be Proud Of

Defining Your New Life

Before you begin to make big changes, it's important to know exactly what kind of life you want. Take some time to ask yourself an important question: What does a life I'm proud of look like? This is not about being perfect or having a lot of money. It's not about making other people happy or getting their approval. Instead, it's about being true to yourself and living with honesty and respect for who you really are.

Understanding Authenticity and Integrity

When we say authenticity, we mean living a life that matches your true feelings and values. Integrity means acting in a way that is honest and fair, even when it's hard. Together, authenticity and integrity create a way of living that makes you feel good about yourself every day. For example, if you want to be honest with your friends and yourself, then making choices that reflect that honesty will help you feel proud when you look in the mirror. This kind of life is not about pretending to be someone you are not. It's about accepting yourself and making choices that reflect that acceptance.

How Do You Want to Feel?

One way to start defining your ideal life is to think about how you want to feel most of the time. Do you want to feel full of energy, like you want to try new things and meet new people? Or do you want to feel peaceful, calm, and happy just being in the moment? Maybe you want to feel curious, always learning and discovering new ideas. Or it could be that you want to feel loved, connected to family, friends, or a community. Think about these feelings carefully. For example, if feeling peaceful is important to you, then you might want to spend time each day relaxing or meditating. If feeling loved is what you want, maybe you'd make an effort to reach out to old friends or spend more time with family.

How Do You Want to Spend Your Days?

Next, consider how you want to use your time each day. Your days are the building blocks of your life, so it's important they reflect your values. What kind of work would you enjoy doing? It might be something creative like painting or writing, or maybe helping others as a teacher or nurse. What about your relationships? Do you want to spend more time with friends or family? Hobbies and free time are important too. Do you want to learn to play music, travel, or take care of your garden? Write down specific ways you could spend your time. For example, if you want to spend your days helping others, you could volunteer at a local food bank or help neighbors with gardening. If you want to learn a hobby, set a goal to practice it for twenty minutes every day.

The Person You Want to Become

Think about the kind of person you want to be in the future. This is about the qualities and habits that make you who you are. Maybe you want to be more patient, so when things get frustrating, you don't lose your calm. Maybe you want to be brave and try new things even when they seem scary. Generosity might be important to you, so you want to help others often, even in small ways. Or creativity could be something you want to grow, by writing stories, drawing, or finding new solutions at work. Try to list a few personal qualities that are important to you. Then, think of simple steps to practice these qualities each day. For patience, that might mean taking deep breaths when you feel upset. For generosity, it could be sharing your lunch or listening carefully when someone talks.

Picture Yourself a Year from Now

Imagine yourself one year from now. Look back and think about the choices you made. What kinds of choices would make you feel good inside? These might be small actions, like exercising regularly or choosing kindness when someone is having a bad day. Consistency is key.

It's not about one big change but many small actions done over time. Maybe you decided to save a small amount of money every week, or you spent time each evening reading to relax. Picture how these small habits add up to a life you are proud of. This helps you understand what really matters and motivates you to keep going.

Creating Your North Star

When you define your ideal life, it helps to think of it as a North Star. A North Star is something that guides you and keeps you on the right track when things get confusing. Your idea of a good life doesn't have to be strict or unchangeable. Instead, it should be flexible and allow room for new opportunities and changes. For example, your North Star might be feeling happy and healthy, but how you get there can change. One day, that might mean going for a walk, and another day, spending time with a friend. Having this kind of guiding light makes it easier to make decisions that feel right and true.

Avoiding Rigidity in Your Life Plan

It is important not to get stuck in thinking your ideal life means one exact way of living. Life changes, and so can your goals. The North Star you set should help you move forward, but not limit you. For example, maybe today you want to be patient and calm, but tomorrow you need to be bold and take risks. Both ways can lead you to a life that feels good. This flexibility helps you deal with changes, challenges, and surprises without feeling lost or frustrated.

Putting It All Together

To start defining your new life, sit down with a notebook or your computer. Write about the feelings you want, the activities you enjoy, and the qualities you want to build in yourself. Don't rush this step. Spend a few days or even weeks thinking about it, adding details as you go. Make a list of small actions you can take that connect to your ideas. Then, check in with yourself regularly. It might help to set a reminder each week to read your notes and see if the steps you are taking match your North Star. This makes your new life plan a living thing that grows with you.

Examples of Small Actions

Here are some examples to help you imagine the small, consistent actions that build your ideal life:

- If feeling peaceful is your goal, try starting each morning with five minutes of deep breathing.

- If curiosity is important, spend fifteen minutes each day reading about something new or watching educational videos.

- To become more generous, set a goal to do one kind thing daily, even if it's as simple as holding a door open.

- If you want to be courageous, try saying yes to one new experience every week, like joining a new club or trying a new food.

- For patience, practice waiting without checking your phone or taking a moment to smile when things get frustrating.

These actions might seem small alone, but together, they create habits that shape your real daily life.

Reflecting on Your Progress

After some time, take a moment to reflect on what you've done and how it feels. Are you becoming the person you want to be? Are your days filled with the feelings you hoped for? If not, don't worry. Go back to your notes and see if your North Star needs some adjusting. This process is about learning and growing, not about being perfect.

By taking these steps, you create a clear and personal idea of a proud life. This helps you make choices that feel right every day, without pressure to be perfect or please others. Your life becomes something you own and enjoy.

Write Down Your Non-Negotiables

Clarity is Strengthened by Boundaries

Having clear boundaries helps you see your life more clearly. Boundaries set limits on what is acceptable and what is not. They give you a framework for how you want to live. When you set these limits, you protect yourself from confusion and feeling overwhelmed. Boundaries help you focus on what is truly important. They create space for your values and goals to be honored every day.

Understanding Non-Negotiables

Non-negotiables are those things you do not compromise on. They are your core values, standards, and conditions that you hold firm no matter what. Think of them as the rules you set for yourself to live by. These are not just wishes or options to consider — they are firm decisions that guide your life. For example, if honesty is a non-negotiable for you, that means you will not accept lies or dishonesty in your relationships.

Examples of Non-Negotiables

Non-negotiables can be very different for every person because everyone values different things. One common example is honesty in relationships. This means you require truthfulness from friends, family, or partners. If someone lies or hides important things, that breaks your boundary and is not acceptable in your life.

Another example is getting enough sleep and rest. Sleep is essential to mental health. If you do not rest enough, you feel tired, stressed, and less able to handle challenges. Saying no to late-night work or commitments that cut into your sleep is a way to protect this non-negotiable.

Work that aligns with your values is also a key non-negotiable for many people. This means choosing jobs or projects that feel meaningful and true to you. For example, if you care deeply about the environment, you might refuse work that harms natural resources. Holding this non-negotiable helps you feel proud and motivated in what you do.

Finally, making time for creativity or connection is important for a balanced life. This could mean scheduling regular time to paint, write, play music, or meet with friends. These activities recharge your spirit and keep you connected to yourself and others.

Writing Down Your Non-Negotiables

Put your non-negotiables in writing. Writing them down makes them real and clear in your mind. When you write a non-negotiable, be specific about what it means. For example, instead of just writing "enough rest," write "I will get at least seven hours of sleep every night." This gives you a clear and measurable standard to follow.

Make your list concrete. Think of it as a list of deal-breakers. These are the things you will not bend on, no matter what challenges come your way. When a situation arises, you can check your list and know right away what decision to make.

The Purpose of Non-Negotiables

Non-negotiables serve two main purposes. The first is to protect you from repeating negative patterns. If you have been in situations that left you feeling bad, remembering your non-negotiables can keep you from going back to them. For example, if in the past you ignored your need for rest and ended up burned out, your non-negotiable about sleep helps you avoid that again.

The second purpose is to help you make decisions quickly and confidently. Life often presents choices where you might feel unsure or guilty. When your non-negotiables are clear, you do not have to guess what to do. For instance, if honesty is non-negotiable, and someone asks you to lie, you know immediately that you will say no. This saves time and reduces stress.

Living in Alignment With Your Non-Negotiables

When you live according to your non-negotiables, your life feels more purposeful. You stop reacting to every situation and begin acting with intention. This does not mean life will be perfect or easy, but it means you have a steady guide to follow.

Imagine your non-negotiables as an anchor. In the storm of uncertainty or change, they keep you grounded. Knowing what you will and will not accept gives you strength. It helps you move forward with more confidence and less doubt.

Taking the time to identify and honor your non-negotiables is a powerful step. It shapes how you interact with people and how you make choices about your time and energy. Each non-negotiable you uphold becomes a building block for a life that feels authentic and steady.

Focus on the Next 6–12 Months, Not Forever

Starting Over Without Feeling Overwhelmed

Starting over can feel really overwhelming. When you think about creating a "perfect" life many years from now, it might seem so far away that it's hard to know where to begin. Instead of focusing on a future that feels distant and unclear, it's better to think about what you can realistically do in the next 6 to 12 months. This shorter time frame makes the whole process feel more manageable and less scary.

Setting Short-Term, Concrete Goals

One important step is to set short-term goals that are clear and easy to understand. These goals should match the kind of life you want to build. It's important to make these goals ambitious enough so they push you, but also realistic enough so you don't give up right away. Goals should be specific, so you can measure your progress. This helps you stay on track without feeling overwhelmed by everything that needs to happen.

For example, if getting healthier is part of your plan, rather than trying to change all your habits overnight, you could focus on something simple like walking for 20 minutes a day or doing a short workout three times a week. This kind of goal is easy to measure. You can keep a calendar or use an app to track each time you complete your routine. When you see the progress, it encourages you to keep going.

Making Small Changes in Relationships

If improving your relationships is part of your vision for a better life, it's helpful to think about small, meaningful actions you can take soon. Try setting a goal like reaching out to a friend or family member once a week to check in, or planning a coffee date or phone call. These little efforts build stronger connections over time. Instead of expecting big changes immediately, focus on making consistent actions that bring people closer.

For example, send a thoughtful message to someone you care about or listen attentively when you spend time with someone. These small things add up and can improve your relationships step by step. It's easy to feel better about your social life when you know you are making positive moves, even if the changes are small at first.

Shifting Careers Step by Step

If changing your career is your goal, it's important to break the process down into smaller parts you can work on over the next six months. Instead of hoping for a total career transformation right away, you could focus on learning new skills, reaching out to people in your desired field, or updating your resume and portfolio.

For instance, spend 30 minutes every day taking an online course related to your new career interest. Join professional groups on social media or attend networking events where you can meet people who work in the field you want to enter. These concrete steps help you build momentum. You gain useful knowledge and connections that can open new doors over time. The key is to keep your efforts steady and focused.

Building Momentum Through Small Wins

Focusing on short-term goals helps you create momentum. When you achieve small victories, like completing your workout three times a week or making a new connection, it feels good. These wins build confidence and show you that progress is possible. Over time, these little successes add up and lead to bigger changes.

For example, if you start by walking daily and stick to it for a few months, you might find yourself naturally wanting to try more challenging exercises. Or if you make new friends and improve your social skills, it can boost your confidence in other areas of life too. Slowly, these small steps begin to change how you think and act.

Changing How You Think and Act

As you focus on small, achievable goals, you'll notice a change in your mindset. When you see yourself making progress, even if it's small, you start believing that a better life is possible. Your actions will also change because you're building good habits. Over time, this new way of thinking and acting will help you move closer to the life you want.

For example, you might start feeling more motivated each day. That motivation can push you to try new things, even if they are outside your comfort zone. You become more open to opportunities and willing to learn from experiences. It all begins with those small goals that are clear and doable in the short term.

Closing Reflection

Clarity is not a single moment of insight — it's a practice.
Define the life that would make you proud, write down your non-negotiables, and commit to what you can do in the next 6–12 months.

When you do this, the path forward becomes less intimidating. Your choices become deliberate, not reactionary. And as you start to live in alignment with what you truly want, the past loses its grip, and the next chapter of your life begins to take shape.

Starting over doesn't have to be a leap into the unknown. It can be a series of intentional steps — small, clear, and focused — that lead you to a life that finally feels like your own.

Chapter 5
Simplify Your Environment

S tarting over isn't just an internal process — it's a physical one too. Our surroundings have a profound effect on our thoughts, emotions, and habits. Clutter, reminders of old patterns, and spaces that no longer serve us can quietly keep us tethered to the past. Simplifying your environment is not about perfection; it's about creating a space that supports your growth, your clarity, and your new life.

Declutter Your Space to Declutter Your Mind

How Our Physical Spaces Reflect Our Mental State

Our surroundings say a lot about what's happening inside our heads. When the places we live and work in are messy or full of stuff we don't need, it can be hard to focus or think clearly. This mess can make us feel stressed or tired because our brains pick up on the chaos and get stuck reacting to it instead of coming up with new ideas. Think about your home, your office, or even the computer screen you use every day. If these areas are overloaded with clutter, it's easy for your mind to feel scattered, like trying to focus with a dozen things pulling at your attention all at once.

Clutter acts like a drain on your energy. Every time you see piles of things around you, your brain has to process that visual noise. This uses up mental power that could be spent on more useful or creative thoughts. Imagine trying to write a story or solve a problem with papers stacked everywhere or notifications blinking on your screen nonstop. Your brain ends up in what's called "reactive mode," which means it's busy responding to distractions instead of being calm and creative. This makes it hard to relax, plan, or get motivated.

Getting Started with Decluttering

The idea of cleaning up your entire space might seem overwhelming. Instead of trying to organize everything at once, pick a small part to focus on first. This could be a single drawer where you keep your office supplies, a bookshelf, or even a corner of your room. When you start small, decluttering feels more manageable and less stressful. You don't have to turn your whole home upside down in one go.

Once you've chosen your spot, take everything out and look at each item carefully. A helpful way to decide what to keep is to ask yourself a few simple questions. For example, "Does this item support the life I am building?" Think about whether the things in front of you help you move toward your goals and the kind of person you want to be. If you have old notebooks full of unfinished ideas or clothes that don't fit anymore, these might not support your current life and could be let go.

Finding Objects That Bring Positive Energy

Another question to consider is, "Does this item spark positive energy, focus, or inspiration?" Some things in your space might make you feel good or help you concentrate better. This could be a plant on your desk, a photo that reminds you of a happy moment, or a favorite mug that makes you smile. Keeping these kinds of items can create a space that feels welcoming and motivates you to do your best work.

If an object doesn't make you feel good or focused, it might be time to put it aside. For example, maybe you have books you never plan to read again, old paperwork, or gadgets you no longer use. These things can weigh on your mind without you even realizing it. When you start removing such items, notice how the space feels different. It often becomes lighter and more open, which can help your brain relax and be more creative.

Letting Go of the Past That Holds You Back

Sometimes, clutter comes from things we keep because of memories or emotions, even if they aren't useful anymore. You might have souvenirs from old relationships, clothes from a time in your life you're ready to move past, or gifts that don't fit your current style. It can be hard to let go of these items because they tie you to a past you're trying to leave behind.

Ask yourself if holding onto these things brings you happiness or just keeps you stuck. For example, if you find a box of letters from an old job that made you unhappy, think about whether reading them helps you learn or if they only bring up old stress. Releasing these items doesn't mean forgetting your past. Instead, it means choosing to focus on where you want to go. When you let go of physical reminders that anchor you to old feelings, you create space for new experiences and goals.

The Real Goal: Mental Clarity

The point of cleaning your space isn't to turn it into a perfect showroom where everything looks like a store display. Instead, the real goal is to clear your mind. Each item you decide to get rid of is like lifting a small weight off your shoulders. When you finish, your space may look simpler, but your head will feel clearer.

Try to notice how you feel during this process. It might not be easy at first, especially if you have a lot of stuff. But as you keep going, you'll find that the physical act of making space around you also makes room inside your mind. With less clutter, you might notice that your ideas flow easier, your mood improves, and your energy increases.

You could think of decluttering as a way to take care of yourself. It's not just about the stuff; it's about how your environment supports you every day. For example, a clean desk might make it easier to start your homework or work project because there are fewer distractions. A tidy corner of your room could become a spot for reading or relaxing, helping you unwind after a long day.

Taking It Step by Step

If the thought of decluttering feels too big, remember that you don't have to do it all at once. You can work slowly over days or weeks. Set a timer for 10 or 15 minutes each day to focus on a small part of your space. Turn on some music if that helps you feel motivated. After you finish, take a moment to appreciate the difference you've made.

Some people find it helpful to sort their things into categories like "keep," "donate," "recycle," and "trash." This makes decisions easier because you don't have to think too hard about what comes next. For example, an old shirt without holes might still be good enough to donate to charity rather than throwing it away. Sorting also helps you make plans for the things you want to give away.

Keep in mind that decluttering your digital space is just as important. Your computer files, email inbox, and phone apps can also get cluttered and make it harder to focus. Try deleting apps you don't use or organizing your files into folders with clear names. You could also unsubscribe from email lists that aren't useful or hide notifications that distract you from your work.

By taking small, steady steps and focusing on keeping only what truly supports you, you create a space that helps your mind feel calm and energized. This makes it easier to do the things you enjoy and reach your goals.

Keep Only What Supports Your New Path

Starting Over with Intentional Choices

When you decide to start over, it means making careful and deliberate choices about the things around you. These choices are not random. They shape the way you live and grow. Every item in your space, every habit you keep, and the routines you follow should have a clear and important purpose. If something in your life does not support your growth or has no meaningful role, it can become a distraction. This means you need to pay attention to what you allow into your daily environment. For example, if you want to improve your health, you might choose to have healthy snacks available rather than junk food. This is a simple, intentional choice that supports your goal.

Identifying What Fits Your New Path

Looking at your surroundings with fresh eyes is an important step. Ask yourself whether each object or habit matches the direction you want to go in your life. For instance, if you want to focus more on creativity, you might keep a journal close by to write down ideas. A vision board with your goals and dreams can serve as a daily reminder to stay motivated. Meaningful books can inspire you, especially if they contain stories or information related to your new path. For example, someone starting a new fitness routine might read books on healthy living or fitness journeys to stay encouraged.

Objects That Inspire and Motivate

Objects that inspire or motivate you play a special role in your environment. A journal is a great example because it allows you to capture thoughts, plan your day, or reflect on your progress. You can write small goals or gratitude lists, which help keep your mindset positive. A vision board is another powerful tool. Making one involves cutting or printing pictures and words that represent your dreams. You then place this board where you see it often. Seeing these reminders regularly can boost your motivation. A meaningful book, such as a biography of someone you admire or a guide to personal growth, provides knowledge and inspiration whenever you need it. These items keep your energy focused on what matters to you now.

Tools to Help You Reach Your Goals

Having the right tools around you makes reaching goals much easier. For example, if a healthier lifestyle is your goal, having cooking utensils you use regularly is a helpful way to support that. You could keep a cutting board, knives, or measuring cups within reach to encourage cooking at home instead of ordering takeout. If you are picking up a new hobby like painting or knitting, supplies organized and ready to use encourage you to spend time on these activities. Having everything in order also saves time because you don't have to search for what you need. When tools are easy to find and use, you are more likely to stick with your new habits until they become part of your routine.

Items That Bring Peace and Joy

It is equally important to have things in your space that make you feel calm and happy. Starting over is not just about work or productivity, but also about rest and peace of mind. These items create a place where you can relax and think clearly. For example, a comfortable chair or a cozy throw blanket can make your favorite reading corner inviting. Plants are another example—they bring a touch of nature indoors and can make your space feel fresh. Soft lighting or candles can add warmth and create a peaceful atmosphere. These small comforts help you recharge and prepare mentally for the challenges ahead.

Letting Go of What No Longer Serves You

Being ruthless with objects and habits that don't support your new life can be difficult, but it's necessary. Keeping things "just in case" ties you to old stories and habits that hold you back. For instance, holding on to clothes that don't fit or that you don't like can clutter your space and mind. Old papers, broken gadgets, or unfinished projects can weigh you down emotionally too. By letting these go, you create space to focus on what truly matters. You don't have to do this all at once. You can start small by picking one drawer or one shelf and clearing out only what is unnecessary. Over time, this builds momentum.

Creating Room for Intention and Growth

When you remove the clutter, whether physical or mental, you open up room for good things. Intention means acting with clear purpose rather than going through the motions. Focusing your environment on your goals helps remind you daily of your reasons for starting over. This kind of focus encourages growth because your surroundings no longer distract or confuse you. For example, if your desk has only the tools you need for work or study, you are less likely to get sidetracked by unrelated things like old mail or random trinkets. This simple act of organizing can improve concentration and productivity over time.

Create a Physical Reset to Match Your Mental One

Simplifying Your Environment as an Ongoing Practice

Simplifying your environment isn't just something you do once and then forget about. It's more like a habit or a ritual that shows the new mental space you are working to create inside yourself. When your surroundings start to feel lighter, calmer, and more in line with what you want to achieve, your mind often begins to feel that way too. It's not just about cleaning or tidying once; it's about regularly making sure your space matches your goals and feelings. This ongoing process can help you feel more peaceful and motivated over time.

For example, instead of just cleaning your desk once, you might decide to spend 10 minutes at the end of each day putting things back where they belong or removing anything that doesn't belong there. Or maybe every weekend, you check one part of your room or your digital space to see if anything is cluttering up your focus.

Creating a "Reset Space" for Mental Clarity

One helpful idea is to create what you can think of as a "reset space." This could be a corner of a room that you set up just for relaxing, thinking, or working on your goals. It might even be a special folder on your computer or phone where you keep important files or ideas that help you stay clear and focused. The key is that this space should feel like a fresh start whenever you use it.

Your reset space should be intentional, meaning it is designed with a clear purpose in mind. It should be a place without distractions — no messy piles of papers, no unnecessary gadgets, or irrelevant decorations. Instead, it should be arranged so that everything there supports clear thinking and focus. If you want, you could decorate this area with a plant, a simple picture, or an object that reminds you why you are making changes in your life. The idea is for this space to reflect the life you want to build, not the past you want to leave behind.

Simple Actions That Can Make a Big Difference

Small changes to your environment can have a surprisingly large impact on how you feel and think. One easy step is to rearrange your furniture in a way that opens up your space. For instance, moving your desk to face the window or shifting the couch to create more walking space can help energy feel freer and your mind feel less crowded. Try moving things around and see how it changes your mood or ability to focus.

Another step is to remove old photographs, posters, or memorabilia that do not inspire you anymore. These items might bring up old memories that don't support your current mindset or goals. You don't have to throw everything away, but think about keeping only those things that make you happy or motivate you to keep moving forward. You might pack away some items in boxes to revisit later or decide to give some things to friends or family who might appreciate them more.

Organizing your digital life is just as important. Delete files you no longer need, unsubscribe from newsletters or email lists that clutter your inbox, and delete apps from your phone that you don't use. Spending a bit of time every week or every month cleaning up emails and messages can free up mental space. For example, use folders to sort important emails and maintain clear labels, or delete photos on your phone that are blurry or no longer useful to you. This kind of digital decluttering helps reduce distractions and makes it easier to find what's really important.

Seeing Your Environment as a Reflection of Your Intentions

When you take these steps, you start to notice how your environment reflects your intentions. A clean, ordered space serves as a reminder that you have chosen to move forward. Each time you enter your reset space or look around your room or digital folders and see clear surfaces, organized files, and items that support your goals, it reinforces your mental reset.

This connection between your environment and your mindset helps you stay committed to your new direction. It's like giving yourself little reminders that you are making progress and have control over your choices. Over time, this can make it easier to stay positive and focused, even when things feel tough.

You might find it helpful to make a habit of spending a few minutes each day or week just noticing your space and asking yourself if it still feels right for where you want to go. If something feels cluttered or distracting, that might be a good sign it's time to tidy, rearrange, or refresh part of your environment again. This ongoing awareness brings you back to the present moment and helps build a mental space that supports growth and calmness.

Closing Reflection

Simplifying your environment is more than a clean-up — it's a declaration. It's saying, *I am ready for something new.* By decluttering your space, keeping only what supports your new path, and creating a physical reset that mirrors your mental one, you give yourself the clarity, energy, and freedom to start over fully.

Your surroundings can either anchor you to your past or lift you into your future. Choose the latter. Let your space breathe, and in doing so, let yourself breathe too.

Chapter 6
Build Micro-Habits

It's easy to feel intimidated when you have to start something anew. The idea of redesigning your life — changing your routines, habits, and mindset — may seem like a massive undertaking. But the truth is, transformation rarely comes from one grand gesture. It comes from consistent, small actions that compound over time. These are called **micro habits**, and they are the secret to sustainable change.

Micro habits are tiny steps that feel almost too small to matter — and that's exactly why they work. They bypass resistance, reduce decision fatigue, and create momentum. Over weeks and months, these small actions accumulate into life-altering results.

Small Daily Actions Compound Faster Than Big Plans

Understanding the Power of Micro Habits

Big plans often get people excited. They imagine huge changes and big results. But many times, these plans don't last. They require a lot of effort, motivation, or willpower. This can make them hard to stick with. Instead of focusing on big changes right away, micro habits offer a simple and steady way forward. These habits focus on being consistent, not intense.

What Are Micro Habits?

Micro habits are tiny actions you do regularly. They may seem small or unimportant at first. But their strength comes from how often you do them. For example, doing one push-up every day looks very easy. It's just one push-up, a short activity that takes only a few seconds. Because it's so small, it's easy not to skip. This small move starts a chain reaction in your daily life.

One Push-Up A Day Example

Let's think about the push-up example. Doing one push-up daily could seem too little to matter. But when you commit to it, something happens. After a few days, you might start feeling stronger. Your body gets used to the movement. The next day, you might do two push-ups. Then three. Soon enough, doing ten push-ups in a row feels normal. This happens without the stress of trying to push through a hard workout from the start. Slowly, your body changes, your mind builds willpower, and your discipline grows—all from one simple habit.

Micro Habits in Reading

Micro habits work well in other areas too. Take reading, for example. If a person reads only one page of a book daily, it doesn't feel like a big task. One page might take just a few minutes. But day by day, those pages add up. By the end of a month, that person may have read a whole book. In a year, they could have finished dozens of books. This happens because they made reading a small and daily habit. There's no pressure to read a whole book at once. The small action becomes part of their daily routine, and the results of that small habit become very big.

Journaling One Sentence Every Day

Journaling is another habit that benefits from this approach. Writing one sentence a day might seem too small to matter. However, this single sentence can start a habit of reflection. After a few weeks, writing daily helps a person think clearly about their feelings and goals. They might stop for a moment each day to write down what they're thankful for or what happened. Over time, their journal fills with thoughts, and they develop better self-understanding and clarity. This idea can make journaling easy to start, maintaining the habit without feeling overwhelmed.

Drinking One Extra Glass of Water Daily

Even simple health habits can be improved by micro habits. Drinking one more glass of water every day can make a big difference. Many people forget to drink enough water and feel tired or sluggish because of it. Starting with just one extra glass a day is easy. For example, someone might decide to drink a glass of water right after waking up or before each meal. Gradually, as they do this every day, their water intake increases naturally. Over time, this helps boost energy, improve skin health, and support overall well-being. It's a small change with a clear, positive effect.

Why Micro Habits Work: The Momentum Effect

The main reason micro habits work so well is momentum. It's much easier to start something small. One push-up, a few words, a sip of water—it doesn't take much willpower. Because the actions are tiny, skipping them feels like missing very little. This makes it harder to ignore the habit. The regularity creates a flow, a rhythm that builds and grows. As you do these small actions consistently, their effects stack up. Each day adds a little more, and over weeks and months, these tiny steps cause big changes.

Why Big Plans Often Fail

In comparison, big plans often try to change too much at once. People might set goals that require hours of work, drastic lifestyle changes, or heavy motivation. This can make the plan feel overwhelming. When motivation drops or life gets busy, it's easy to give up. Big plans can collapse under their own weight because they are too hard to keep going day by day. Micro habits prevent this because they remove the pressure of huge effort and replace it with easy, small moves.

How to Start Your Own Micro Habits

Starting micro habits is simple but requires some planning. First, choose one small action that feels doable. Make sure it's something you can do every day, no matter what. For example, if you want to start exercising, pick one push-up or one stretch. If you want to read more, pick reading one page or even one paragraph. Set a specific time to do your habit, like right after brushing your teeth or while waiting for coffee to brew. This helps make the habit part of your daily routine.

Another important step is tracking your progress. You can keep a simple checklist or use a calendar. Cross off each day that you do your habit. Seeing those marks or ticks can motivate you to keep going. After some time, the habit will require less effort because it becomes automatic.

How to Grow Micro Habits Over Time

Once your micro habit feels easy, you can slowly increase it. If you started with one push-up, try two or three after a few weeks. If one page of reading feels manageable, try adding more pages when it feels right. This gentle increase helps build strength, knowledge, or other benefits without overwhelming you. Because the habit is already in place, growing it feels natural.

Examples from Real Life

Many people use this approach to reach their goals. For instance, people trying to improve their fitness might begin with just a few minutes of walking daily. Over weeks, they increase their speed and distance. Writers often start by writing just one sentence a day. Over time, their sentences become paragraphs, then pages. Learning new skills, like playing an instrument or cooking, also works well with micro habits. Starting just five minutes a day creates steady progress that lasts.

Summary of Micro Habit Benefits

Micro habits keep things simple. They make it easy to start and keep going. They avoid the stress of big efforts and reduce the chance of failure. By focusing on small actions and consistency, micro habits build momentum. This momentum results in noticeable changes over time. They are a powerful way to make progress without pressure or burnout.

Start With One Keystone Habit

Understanding Keystone Habits

A keystone habit is a simple habit that can start a chain reaction, helping you make many positive changes in your life. Instead of trying to change everything at once and feeling overwhelmed, focusing on one small habit can make things easier. This small habit sets the tone for other improvements. When you build one good habit, it often encourages you to start other helpful habits naturally. The effects spread out like ripples in a pond, making many parts of your life better over time.

The Power of Prioritizing Sleep

Sleep is one of the most important keystone habits you can have. By making sure you get enough rest, you improve many things like your mood, energy, focus, and the decisions you make. Even small changes, like going to bed 15 minutes earlier, can make a big difference. For example, if you usually go to bed at 11:00 PM, try going to bed at 10:45 PM instead. This small change might not seem like much, but it helps your body and mind recharge better.

When you sleep well, you feel less tired the next day. This makes it easier to concentrate and avoid feeling grumpy or stressed. That extra energy can help you eat healthier meals, because you have more willpower and better judgment. It also makes it more likely that you will exercise or spend time being productive. Sleep affects many parts of your life, so improving your rest can start a positive chain reaction.

How Movement Sparks Change

Movement is another strong keystone habit. It does not mean you need to spend hours in the gym. Even a short daily walk or a few stretches can help your body and mind feel better. For example, try walking around your neighborhood for 10 minutes each day. Or spend five minutes stretching your arms and legs when you wake up or before bed. Small amounts of movement make your muscles stronger and improve your mood.

When you move regularly, your confidence can grow. Feeling stronger and healthier often makes you want to keep moving and try other healthy habits. You might start eating better to support your workouts or set goals to walk farther. Movement also helps reduce stress and clear your mind. This can make it easier to focus and get things done throughout the day. When one habit gets started, it can lead to many others naturally.

Journaling: A Keystone Habit for the Mind

Journaling is a habit where you write down your thoughts, goals, or things you are thankful for. This simple action helps clarify your mind and reduce anxiety. If you feel overwhelmed, writing things out can make problems seem smaller and easier to manage. For example, try spending five minutes each morning writing about what you want to achieve that day or what you appreciate in your life.

Writing can also help you track your progress and keep your focus on what matters most. By putting your goals on paper, you create a clear path to follow. This can increase your productivity because you know exactly what to do next. Journaling encourages you to be honest with yourself and notice what is working or not working in your habits. As you write regularly, you become more motivated and better organized.

Anchoring Your Keystone Habit in Daily Life

Choose one keystone habit to start with and make it part of your everyday routine. It helps to pick something small and doable so you don't feel discouraged. For example, if you pick sleep, decide on a specific time to go to bed every night and stick to it. If you choose movement, set a daily reminder to walk or stretch, even if it is only for five minutes.

As the habit becomes automatic, it will start to make other good habits easier. When you sleep better, you might notice you want to eat more fruits and vegetables or plan your meals. When you journal, you may find your work or study time becomes more focused. When you move daily, your confidence might grow, encouraging you to try new activities or improve your diet.

The key is to let this habit become a foundation. It supports other habits naturally without forcing yourself. Over time, these changes can add up to a healthier and more balanced life. Instead of overwhelming yourself with many goals, start with one small keystone habit and watch how it helps improve everything else.

Make Habits So Small They're Hard to Skip

The Magic of Micro Habits Lies in Simplicity

Habits that seem too big can feel overwhelming, making you want to avoid them. When you look at a goal and it feels hard or like it will take a lot of effort, it's easy to put it off or give up. But when a habit feels easy and small, you are more likely to do it, even on days when you feel tired or unmotivated. The idea behind micro habits is to keep things very simple so that the habit doesn't become a struggle. This way, the habit fits smoothly into your daily life without creating stress or pressure.

Make Your Habit So Small It's Almost Impossible to Skip

A good way to start is by making your habit so small that skipping it feels weird or unlikely. When something is very easy to do, it's much easier to keep doing it regularly. If your habit is tiny, it doesn't take much time or energy. This small start can help you build momentum for bigger changes later. For example, instead of telling yourself that you will meditate for 20 minutes every day, start with just one minute of focused breathing. This one minute can be as simple as sitting quietly and paying attention to your breath. This tiny action feels doable, and once you do it, it's easier to continue.

Example: Meditation

Say you want to begin meditating. If you try to meditate for 20 minutes right away, it might feel too hard. You could get distracted or feel like you don't have time. But if you commit to meditating for only 1 minute, it is much easier to make it a habit. You can set a timer on your phone for one minute, sit quietly, and focus on your breath. After a few days, you might find yourself naturally wanting to meditate longer because it feels good and not like a chore.

Example: Exercise

Exercise is another good example. Many people want to exercise for an hour every day, but that can feel intimidating and time-consuming. Instead, commit to doing just five push-ups or take a two-minute walk. It sounds so small that it doesn't feel like a big commitment. The key is to do it every day. When you do those five push-ups or short walks consistently, your body starts to enjoy moving more. Over time, these tiny steps can lead to longer workouts because you've built the habit first.

Example: Writing

Writing in a journal or working on creative writing can also start small. Instead of trying to write a full page every day, start by writing one sentence. This tiny goal lowers the resistance to starting because it feels easy. You can write one sentence about your day, your thoughts, or anything on your mind. Once you start writing that one sentence, sometimes you'll want to keep going and write more. This approach allows you to build the habit without feeling pressured.

The Goal Is Consistency, Not Perfection or Intensity

When working on habits, the most important thing is to be consistent, not perfect. It's better to do a tiny habit every day than to push yourself too hard and quit after a few days. When a habit is very small and easy, you won't fail easily. That makes it unstoppable. Each day that you do the habit adds up to progress over time. The habit becomes a part of your daily routine and feels automatic.

For example, if you try to meditate for 20 minutes but skip several days, you might get discouraged. But if you meditate for one minute every day, it's hard to imagine missing it. This consistency builds your confidence. You start seeing yourself as someone who sticks to habits, and that feeling motivates you to keep going.

Small Victories Add Up Over Time

When you keep doing these small habits, you build many small victories. Each time you do your habit, you prove to yourself that you can do it. These wins increase your confidence and encourage you to do more. Eventually, the small habits can grow naturally into bigger habits because the base is already there.

For example, if you start walking for two minutes every day and enjoy it, you might find yourself walking for five minutes, then ten minutes, and so on. The original habit was so small that it didn't feel like a big effort, but it created a foundation for bigger change.

How to Start Your Own Micro Habits

- Choose a habit you want to build.

- Shrink it down to the smallest possible action. Make it so easy that you don't want to skip it.

- Do the habit immediately when you can. For example, right after you brush your teeth or before you have breakfast.

- Be patient. Focus on doing it every day, even if it's tiny.

- Celebrate your wins, no matter how small.

- Watch as the habit becomes part of your daily routine and grows on its own.

By keeping habits small and simple, you reduce the chance of failure. Over time, your life will change in meaningful ways without feeling like a struggle.

Closing Reflection

Micro habits are the bridge between intention and transformation. They allow you to start over without feeling overwhelmed, to take action without fear, and to rebuild your life one tiny step at a time.

Remember:

- Small daily actions compound faster than big plans.

- One keystone habit can spark change across your life.

- Make habits so small they're almost impossible to skip.

Starting over doesn't require massive effort — it requires **momentum**, patience, and consistency. Focus on the tiniest steps today, and over weeks and months, you'll look back and realize you've built a life you never thought possible — all from the smallest, most manageable actions.

Chapter 7

Rebuild Your Confidence

S tarting over isn't just about creating new habits or clearing space in your life. It's about reclaiming something that may have been shaken or lost along the way: your confidence. Confidence isn't built in a single dramatic moment; it grows quietly, from repeated experiences of showing up for yourself.

When life falls apart, it's easy to feel small, powerless, or uncertain. Rebuilding your confidence is about restoring faith in your own ability to handle what comes next — one small, intentional step at a time.

Keep Small Promises to Yourself Daily

Confidence Starts with Trust

Confidence is something many people want, but it doesn't just appear out of nowhere. It all begins with trust. Trust is the feeling that you can depend on someone, and in this case, that someone is yourself. When you trust yourself, you feel stronger and more capable of handling whatever life throws at you. But how do you build trust in yourself? The answer lies in keeping promises you make to yourself. When you say you will do something and then follow through, you are proving to yourself that you are reliable. This builds trust little by little.

Keeping Simple Promises

You don't need to start with huge promises. In fact, starting small can be the best way to begin building trust. Simple promises are easier to keep, and each time you do, you build your confidence. For example, you might promise yourself, "I will make my bed each morning." This is a task that doesn't take much time, but when you do it daily, it feels like a win. Another example is promising to "write one sentence in my journal today." Writing just one sentence is not hard and is a way to get into the habit of reflection. Or you could say, "I will take a 5-minute walk." This small action helps you move your body and take a short break, which is good for your mind and health.

How Small Victories Build Self-Reliance

Every time you keep one of these promises, no matter how small it seems, you are telling yourself, "I can trust me." This message is powerful. It reminds you that you can rely on yourself to do what you say you will do. Over time, these tiny wins add up. They become the strong foundation you need to aim for bigger goals. Imagine stacking small blocks to build a tower. Each block alone is small, but together they create something tall and sturdy. In the same way, small acts of keeping promises create a solid base of self-trust. When you believe in yourself, you are more willing to try new things and face challenges. You know that even if things get hard, your word to yourself is important.

The Power of Daily Commitments

It is easy to think that small actions don't matter much. But these daily commitments are very important. They are the bricks that make up a confident and empowered life. For example, if you consistently make your bed each morning, you start the day with a sense of order and accomplishment. When you know you can complete simple tasks, your mind is more ready to take on harder ones. Keeping a promise to go for a short walk every day helps your body stay active and your brain clear. This simple act can also calm your mind, reduce stress, and improve your mood. Writing a single sentence in your journal helps you organize your thoughts and reflect on your day, which can give you better self-awareness.

Practical Steps to Build Trust Through Promises

To start building trust with yourself, pick one small promise that feels doable. Write it down on a note or set a reminder on your phone. For the promise to be effective, it should be something clear and specific, like "I will drink a glass of water first thing after waking up." When the time comes, do the action, even if you don't feel like it. If you miss a day, don't give up. Notice what made you skip it and think about how to make it easier next time. Maybe set your glass of water next to your bed the night before. After following through with this promise for a week or so, add another small promise. Keep them simple and separate so you do not feel overwhelmed.

Understanding Why Keeping Promises Matters

When you keep promises to others, you build trust with them, but when you keep promises to yourself, you build trust deeper inside. This inner trust supports your confidence because it shows you that you are dependable and strong. If you keep breaking promises, even small ones, it can make you doubt yourself and lower your confidence. For example, if you tell yourself you will write one sentence in your journal but never do it, you might start thinking, "I don't follow through on anything." This thought can lead to feeling stuck or unmotivated. On the other hand, keeping promises gives you a sense of achievement and proof that you can set goals and meet them.

Examples of Simple Commitments to Try

Apart from making your bed, writing in your journal, or taking a walk, there are many other small promises you can make to yourself. You could say, "*I will drink a cup of tea without any distractions,*" to practice mindfulness. Or, "*I will smile at myself in the mirror each morning,*" which may help improve mood. Another example is, "*I will spend 2 minutes stretching before bed.*" These simple acts focus on caring for yourself and your well-being. The goal is not to overwhelm yourself but to build a steady rhythm of self-trust.

The Role of Consistency

The key to growing trust and confidence is doing these small actions regularly. Consistency is what turns keeping a promise from a one-time act into a habit. Habits are behaviors that become automatic because you do them so often. When you make your bed every day, it becomes a habit that you don't have to think much about. The same is true for other small promises you keep. Over time, these habits create a lifestyle where you trust yourself naturally. You don't have to force confidence; it grows from everyday trusted actions.

How to Handle Challenges and Setbacks

Sometimes, life gets busy or hard, and you might miss keeping a promise. This is normal, and it does not mean you failed. What matters is how you respond. Instead of being hard on yourself, acknowledge what happened and think about how to get back on track. For example, if you promised to take a 5-minute walk but it didn't happen because of rain, you could promise to walk inside or do gentle stretching instead. Changing the promise to fit your situation still keeps your trust in yourself intact. Being flexible and kind to yourself helps maintain the habit of keeping promises over time.

Growing Confidence Gradually

Confidence does not appear overnight. It is something you build a little at a time. By starting with small promises and keeping them, you create an inner trust. This trust then supports you as you take on bigger challenges. For example, if you want to learn to cook or start a new hobby, you might begin by promising to try one new recipe a week or spend 10 minutes practicing something new every day. Because you have already built trust through smaller promises, you will feel more sure that you can follow through on these bigger goals. This gradual growth makes confidence real and lasting.

Trusting Yourself Means You Can Rely on Your Own Actions

Trusting yourself means believing that you will do what you say you will do. This makes you feel safe and steady inside. When you trust yourself, you don't depend on others to motivate you all the time. Instead, you have a steady source of strength from within. This helps you handle failures better because you know you can keep trying and stay true to your promises.

Creating a Habit of Self-Trust Every Day

The best way to create self-trust is to make promises you can keep every day. Start your morning with one small promise, do it, and feel good about completing it. Then repeat the next day. Over time, you will notice that these simple actions give you a sense of control and confidence. Self-trust turns into a habit, and with it, your confidence grows naturally. This habit is what prepares you for success in other areas of your life because you have already proven you can depend on yourself.

Focus on Progress, Not Perfection

Understanding the Impact of Perfectionism on Confidence

One of the quickest ways to damage your confidence is by expecting yourself to be perfect all the time. When your focus is only on your flaws, the mistakes you make, or the things you didn't do well enough, it's easy to lose sight of how far you've come. Instead of noticing the progress you have achieved, you get caught up in what is missing or not quite right. This can make you feel like you are never good enough, which slowly eats away at your belief in yourself. Real confidence doesn't come from doing everything perfectly. It comes from making steady progress, even if things get messy or don't turn out as planned.

The Power of Celebrating Small Wins

One helpful way to build your confidence is to celebrate the small victories in your daily life. These are the moments when you take a step forward, even if it doesn't seem like a big deal to others. For example, if there is a task you have been putting off, and you finally decide to complete it, that counts as progress. Finishing something you avoided before sends a message to yourself that you can overcome challenges and take action. This helps you feel stronger and more capable.

Another example is when you manage to show up for yourself despite feeling scared or uncomfortable. Maybe you had to speak in front of a group or try something new, and even though it was tough, you did it anyway. That's an important win because it means you are facing your fears and growing. When you acknowledge these moments, no matter how small, you slowly start to believe in your ability to handle difficult situations.

Trying Again After Failure

Failing at something can feel discouraging, but trying again after failure is a major sign of strength. If you did not succeed yesterday but decided to give it another shot today, that is progress. Each time you get back up and try again, you are building resilience. This is the ability to bounce back from setbacks without losing hope. Resilience is a key part of confidence because it shows that you are not defined by your failures but by your determination to keep going.

When you recognize trying after failing as progress, it helps you move away from the idea that success means never making mistakes. Instead, you understand that success involves learning from your errors and improving over time. This mindset encourages you to take risks and grow rather than being stuck by fear of failing.

Measuring Success Through Growth

It is important to change how you measure success if you want your confidence to grow naturally. Instead of setting the bar at being flawless or perfect, try to see success as any kind of growth or improvement. Growth means you are learning new things, adapting, and becoming a better version of yourself, little by little.

For example, if you are learning a new skill like playing the guitar, don't expect to play perfectly right away. Celebrate being able to play one chord cleanly or remember a song's rhythm. These small signs of progress show that you are moving in the right direction. When you look at success this way, confidence starts to build because you see yourself making real advancements.

The Connection Between Progress and Confidence

Progress acts as a reminder that you are capable of change and improvement. It tells you that you have inner strength and persistence. By focusing on progress, you begin to notice that you are not stuck or failing; instead, you are evolving. This kind of thinking encourages you to keep going, even when life feels difficult or imperfect.

Think about a time when you had a rough day but still managed to complete a small task or take a positive step. When you remind yourself of these moments, it becomes easier to trust yourself. You realize that you have handled challenges before, and you can do it again.

Turning Progress Into a Habit

Making a habit of noticing your progress can have a lasting effect on your confidence. One way to do this is by keeping a journal where you write down your achievements each day. These don't need to be big things. It can be something as simple as waking up on time, making a healthy meal, or speaking kindly to yourself. Writing these down helps you see how much you are doing and moving forward.

Another method is to share your small wins with a friend or family member who can support and encourage you. Talking about your progress helps you feel recognized and reinforces the positive changes you are making.

Practical Steps to Embrace Progress Over Perfection

Start by setting realistic goals that focus on effort rather than perfect results. For instance, if you want to get fit, aim to exercise for 15 minutes a day instead of expecting to run five miles immediately. When you reach this goal, celebrate that achievement. Next, gradually increase your effort as your confidence grows.

When you catch yourself thinking you need to be perfect, pause and remind yourself that progress is more important. Practice saying things like "I am getting better" or "It's okay to make mistakes." These simple affirmations can shift your mindset toward growth.

Lastly, make time regularly to review what you have accomplished. Reflect on how far you have come instead of how far you still need to go.

This simple habit helps keep your confidence strong because it focuses your attention on success rather than shortcomings.

Remember Who You Were Before Things Changed

Reconnecting with Your Former Self

When life throws unexpected challenges your way, it can be easy to feel lost or uncertain about who you are. Rebuilding confidence means going back to who you were before things changed. This doesn't mean you ignore the difficulties or pretend they didn't happen. Instead, it means remembering the person you were and understanding that parts of that person are still inside you.

Many times, setbacks make us think we've lost everything good about ourselves. But the truth is, the skills, talents, and strengths you had before are still with you. These are the parts of you that helped you get through hard times in the past. Reconnecting with these parts can help you find your footing again.

Reflecting on Your Past Self

Taking time to think about your past self is really important. Think about who you were before your life changed. What did you enjoy doing? What skills did you have? Maybe you were good at solving problems, being patient, or staying calm under pressure. These qualities don't disappear just because something difficult happened.

You can try this reflection by writing down answers to simple questions. For example, ask yourself: Who was I before this challenge? What were my strengths? What did I care about? Write down as many things as come to mind, even if you think they don't seem important now. This list can help remind you of who you are beyond the current situation.

Recognizing Skills and Passions That Remain

Once you've thought about your past, look at the qualities, skills, or interests that are still part of you today. Maybe you loved painting, writing, or organizing events. Or perhaps you were someone people came to for advice because you were a good listener.

Even if you haven't done these things recently, the desire and ability are likely still inside. For example, if you used to enjoy running or playing sports, you might still have that energy and determination. You can start small by doing one activity again that you once enjoyed, like taking a short walk or sketching something simple. This small step can reconnect you with a sense of who you are.

Remembering Past Challenges You've Overcome

Everyone faces difficulties at some point. Think back to other challenges you have faced before the current one. What were they? How did you handle them? Maybe you dealt with a tough job, a hard school year, or problems with friends or family.

Remembering these past experiences is important because it shows you have dealt with serious problems before and come through them. This experience is a kind of proof that you can handle hard times. Even if things feel overwhelming now, the fact that you've survived and grown from earlier difficulties means you have more strength than you might realize.

Try to write or talk about one or two times in your life when things were hard but you managed to get through. Reflect on what you did during those times. Did you ask for help? Did you find new solutions? Did you take breaks to rest? Understanding what worked before can help you face your current challenges.

Reclaiming Your Confidence

Remembering your past self is not about living in the past or wishing everything could go back to how it was. Instead, it is about using the past as proof of your strength and ability. When you look back at times when you succeeded or managed complex situations, you gather evidence of your competence.

Think of this like building a foundation. Your past experiences, skills, and passions are the bricks. Even if the situation today feels shaky, this foundation is still there. You can stand on it and build again.

If you need a practical way to do this, try creating a "strengths journal." Each day, write down something you did well or a positive quality you noticed in yourself. Over time, this will remind you that you are capable and strong, even if progress feels slow.

Small Steps to Move Forward

Rebuilding confidence doesn't happen in one day. It takes time and small actions. Start by identifying one skill or interest from your past that you feel you would like to reconnect with. For example, if you enjoyed writing before, try writing a short paragraph each day about something simple.

Set small goals that are easy to reach. For instance, if you used to enjoy cooking, try making one new recipe each week. Accomplishing these tasks helps rebuild a sense of achievement, which is important for confidence.

It also helps to reach out to supportive people who encourage you. Talk with friends or family members about your past interests or strengths. Sometimes having someone remind us of our good qualities can make it easier to see them ourselves.

Facing Uncertainty with Past Strengths

Life often brings times where the future feels unclear. This can shake anyone's confidence. But remember, you have dealt with uncertainty before. You have made choices, adapted, and kept moving forward. You have the ability to learn from mistakes and keep trying.

Facing uncertainty is easier when you remind yourself of the tools you already have. These tools could be things like patience, problem-solving skills, or the ability to stay calm when things feel confusing. These are strengths you used before, and you can use them again.

If you want a concrete step to handle uncertainty, try breaking down big problems into smaller parts. Focus on one small thing at a time. This makes things more manageable and can reduce feelings of being overwhelmed.

Using Your Past to Help Now

In summary, reconnecting with your past self helps you remember your value and strength. You are not defined only by the hard things happening now. You are also defined by the skills, experiences, and passions that have shaped you over time.

Use this connection to take slow, steady steps toward regaining your confidence. Reflect on who you were, recognize your remaining strengths, recall past victories, and take small actions to rebuild your sense of self. This process can help you move forward with a better understanding of what you are capable of in the face of current challenges.

Closing Reflection

Confidence is not something you magically regain overnight. It's built through the daily practice of trusting yourself, valuing progress over perfection, and reconnecting with the strengths you already possess.

Start small: keep promises to yourself, honor the steps you take, and remind yourself of the person you were before the storm. Each act, each reflection, each small win chips away at self-doubt, replacing it with quiet certainty and inner strength.

Rebuilding your confidence isn't about proving yourself to anyone else — it's about proving to yourself that you are capable, resilient, and worthy of the life you're now choosing to create.

Part IV
Redefinition
Discovering New Identity & Purpose

Chapter 8
Redefine Your Identity

R ebuilding a new life isn't just about changing your circumstances — it's about changing your sense of self. When life shifts, we often cling to old identities, labels, or roles because they feel safe or familiar. But the truth is, who you were before does not have to define who you are now. Rebuilding your life begins with redefining who you are and who you want to become.

You're Not Who You Were, and That's Okay

Understanding Change in Yourself

It is common to feel ashamed or confused when you notice that your past self does not match the new direction you are taking in life. This feeling can come with questions like, "Am I still the same person?" or "Have I lost who I really am?" It's important to realize that you have not lost yourself. Instead, what you are experiencing is a form of change. Change means that you are growing into someone new, someone who suits the person you want to become. This growth is not about staying the same but about becoming better and more aligned with your true goals.

Sometimes, people fear change because they think it means forgetting or betraying their past. However, change isn't about discarding everything you once were. It's more about choosing to keep the parts of yourself that help you and letting go of those that do not. For example, if you used to have a habit of procrastinating but now you want to be more productive, giving up that habit doesn't erase your past. It shows that you want to improve and be more responsible for your time. This act of transformation honors the future you are aiming for rather than undermining your history.

Shedding Old Habits and Beliefs

Growth involves changing some of your habits, beliefs, and ways of doing things, especially those that no longer suit your life or goals. These habits might be things like certain routines, attitudes, or even the way you think about yourself and others. For instance, if you used to believe that you couldn't succeed in a particular area, easing away from that belief opens the door to new possibilities. You don't become a different person by cheating your past; instead, you make space for new opportunities by letting go of old limitations.

If there was a habit that caused you harm or stopped you from moving forward, it's perfectly okay to leave it behind. This might mean quitting a bad habit like smoking, or changing how you interact with other people. The important thing is to know that changing these parts isn't a betrayal. It's a sign that you want to be healthier and happier in the long run. You are choosing to respect your future self by making these changes.

Accepting Your New Self

One of the most freeing moments in growth happens when you accept that you are no longer the same person you used to be. Accepting this truth opens you to new freedom. It means you don't have to feel bad or guilty for making mistakes before or for having been different. Many times, people hold on to old versions of themselves because they are afraid of what others might think or because they feel guilt about past actions. But realizing that you can move past those feelings is a powerful step.

Taking this acceptance seriously means you stop trying to fit into a box you have already outgrown. Often, people try to act or live as if they are still that old version, but this only brings confusion and frustration. When you accept that you are different now, you give yourself permission to build the life that fits who you are today. You might find that your interests, values, or daily habits change, and that is completely natural.

Letting Go of Guilt

Release of guilt is one of the first things you can do when you understand growth. Guilt often ties you to past mistakes and can keep you stuck in old patterns of thinking. Imagine if you made a mistake years ago, like saying something hurtful or missing an important opportunity. Holding onto guilt makes you judge yourself unfairly and stops you from moving forward.

Instead of staying trapped by guilt, practice forgiving yourself. This could be done by writing down what happened and why it was a mistake, then reminding yourself that mistakes are part of being human. You might say to yourself, "I did the best I could then, and now I am trying to learn and be better." Letting go of guilt is an important action step because it clears your mind and heart for new growth.

Building Confidence in the Present

Once you accept your new self and let go of guilt, the next step is to build confidence in the life you are creating now. Confidence doesn't mean you won't have doubts or fears, but it means you trust your ability to face challenges and make decisions. Confidence comes with practice. For example, start by setting small goals each day, like finishing a task on time or speaking kindly to yourself when you notice criticism.

When you take these steps, you begin to see yourself as someone capable and worthy of success. Daily habits like writing in a journal about your progress, sharing your goals with a trusted friend, or celebrating small wins can help strengthen your confidence. By focusing on who you are now rather than who you used to be, you create a stronger foundation for your future.

Seeing Change as Strength

Many people think change means failure. They might believe that if they change, they haven't succeeded or stayed true to themselves. This is not true. Change is actually a sign of strength. It shows that you are able to face difficulties, learn from them, and keep moving forward. Being able to change takes courage because it means stepping into the unknown.

Think about times in your life when you had to adapt to new situations, such as starting a new job, moving to a new city, or ending a relationship. Each of those moments required bravery and resilience. Recognizing that change is a form of growth helps you respect yourself more and be patient with the process. It shows that you are not giving up; you are preparing yourself for a better future by growing through your experiences.

Let Go of Old Labels and Roles That No Longer Fit

Understanding Labels and Roles

Labels and roles are parts of how we see ourselves and how others see us. A label might be a simple word or phrase that describes us, like "the responsible one" or "the caretaker." A role is the part we play in our families, workplaces, or communities. These labels and roles can be comforting because they help people understand us quickly. For example, if you are known as "the responsible one," others might expect you to always handle important tasks or solve problems. This can be helpful because it gives others a clear idea of who you are and what to expect from you. Labels and roles act like signposts, helping us find our way through the world.

When Labels and Roles Become Limiting

Sometimes, these labels or roles stop being helpful and start holding us back. Maybe you were called "the caretaker" because you looked after your siblings as a child. That label might have made sense then, but as you grow, you might want to explore other sides of yourself. If you keep clinging to the old label, you might feel stuck. You might not try new things or show parts of yourself that do not fit that role. For example, if you always see yourself as the responsible one, you might avoid taking risks or doing things that seem silly even if they would make you happy. Old labels can trap us in stories that no longer fit. They can stop us from growing.

Questions to Reflect On

It helps to ask yourself certain questions when you wonder if labels or roles are holding you back. First, ask, "*Which labels keep me small or stuck?*" Think about the words you use to describe yourself. Are there any that make you feel limited? Maybe you call yourself "shy," and because of that, you avoid speaking up even if you have ideas to share. Or you might label yourself "a failure" after making a mistake. These kinds of labels make it harder to try again or to grow. Recognizing these kinds of labels is the first step in letting them go.

Another question is, "*Which roles prevent me from exploring who I really want to become?*" We often take on roles because of others' expectations. For instance, if you are always seen as "the caretaker," you might find it hard to focus on your own needs and dreams. This role can make you feel obligated to put others first all the time. But what if you want to explore a new career or learn a new hobby? You might feel stuck because the role says you should be busy taking care of others. Highlighting these conflicts can help you see where change is needed.

Finally, ask yourself, "*What identities do I feel pressured to maintain, even if they no longer fit?*" Sometimes family, friends, or work expect us to act a certain way. You might feel that you must keep a label even if it doesn't feel right anymore. For example, your family might expect you to be "the responsible child," always making good choices. While this might have worked when you were a teen, maybe you want to be a bit more carefree now. This pressure can feel heavy and stop you from being true to yourself.

The Power of Letting Go

Letting go of old labels and roles does not make you less of a person. On the contrary, it can open up new possibilities. Imagine carrying a heavy coat on a warm day. It weighs you down and makes moving harder. Labels and roles can be like that heavy coat. When you shed them, you feel lighter and more free. This freedom means you can try new things and grow in ways you might not have before. For example, if you stop telling yourself you are always "the responsible one," you might try a hobby that's just for fun and not anything practical.

To let go, you can start with small steps. Notice when a label or role shows up in your thoughts. When you think, "I'm not good at this because I'm shy," try to challenge that thought. Remind yourself that being shy does not mean you cannot speak up. You can practice sharing your ideas in small, safe groups until you feel more confident. Another step is to try new activities or roles that feel interesting, even if they don't match your old labels. Maybe join a club, take a class, or volunteer. These actions help you explore new parts of yourself.

Redefining Yourself on Your Own Terms

The journey of changing how you see yourself is personal. It takes time and patience. You get to decide which labels and roles fit who you want to be now, not who you were before or who others expect you to be. For instance, if you once saw yourself as "the quiet one," but now want to be more outgoing, start by setting small goals. Say hello to a new person each day or share a thought in a group conversation. Celebrate these small steps as they are part of your growth.

Remember that it is okay to try on different identities. You might explore being creative by painting or writing. Or try being a leader by organizing a project at work or school. Each new experience helps you understand what feels right and authentic. Keeping an open mind allows you to change and redefine yourself without fear.

Moving Toward an Authentic Life

When you remove old labels, you create space for an authentic life—a life that fits who you truly are today. This means being honest with yourself about your feelings and desires. Perhaps you realize you want to be more adventurous or express emotions more openly. It might feel strange or scary at first because you are breaking old patterns. But this change can bring more happiness and satisfaction.

In this process, it's helpful to have support. Talk with friends or family who respect your changes. Find people who encourage your growth. Sometimes writing in a journal about your feelings and experiences can also clarify what you want. The important thing is to be kind to yourself as you learn and grow.

Final Thoughts on Labels and Roles

Labels and roles are parts of us, but they do not have to define us forever. They can change as we change. The key is to be aware of how they affect us. By asking the right questions and taking small steps, we can move beyond old stories and discover new parts of ourselves. This makes life lighter, richer, and more fulfilling.

Choose Values That Align With Your Next Chapter

Redefining Your Identity Through Values

Changing who you are does not mean wiping the slate clean and starting from scratch. Rather, it's about picking the core values that will guide you going forward. Values are like a compass that points you in the right direction. They help you decide what is important and shape how you act in daily life. These values become the strong base on which your new self is built.

Taking Time to Reflect on Your Values

It is important to slow down and think carefully about what really matters to you. Ask yourself some key questions. First, think about the principles you want to live by in the future. Principles are the beliefs or rules that help you make good choices. For example, honesty, kindness, or responsibility can be principles you choose to follow every day.

Next, consider which values will support the kind of life you want to build. If you want a calm and happy life, valuing patience and self-care can help. If you aim for success in your job, values like hard work and persistence might be important. It helps to write these down and explain why each value matters. Writing makes your feelings clearer.

Also, think about how you want to act in different parts of your life. Your relationships with family and friends might need one set of values, such as respect and listening carefully. At work, being professional and reliable could be key. For personal growth, you may choose values like learning new things or staying open to change. When you think about these areas separately, it becomes easier to understand the values you want to keep.

Aligning Your Identity with Your Values

When your identity matches the values you have chosen, you begin to live with purpose. Instead of reacting without thought, you act intentionally. For example, if one of your values is kindness, you might choose to help someone even if you are busy. This kind of action reflects your true self.

Living by your values also gives more meaning to your choices. Every decision, big or small, becomes clearer because it fits with the values you believe in. If honesty is important to you, you will find it easier to tell the truth, even when it is hard.

This consistency in your actions builds confidence. You can trust yourself because your choices come from your real beliefs. When your values and actions line up, your mind feels less confused. You become more sure about who you are and what you want.

Integrating Your Past with Your New Identity

Redefining yourself does not mean forgetting where you came from. Your past experiences shape you in many ways. Instead of erasing your history, try to include the lessons you have learned. Look back and think about the moments that taught you important things. These can be successes and failures, happy times and challenges.

By accepting your past, you honor your journey so far. At the same time, you can make a clear choice to move forward as the person you want to be. This means you decide to be guided by your chosen values, even if they are different from how you acted before.

For example, you may have made mistakes in the past because you didn't value patience. Now, if patience is a value you want to live by, you can practice it every day. This helps you change without losing yourself.

Practical Steps to Choose and Live by Your Values

- Start by listing values that feel important to you. Some common values include honesty, respect, courage, creativity, fairness, and loyalty. Don't rush—take your time to find the best fit.

- Next, test your values in real life. Choose one or two to focus on each week. If patience is a value you want, try practicing it by waiting calmly when things don't go your way. Notice how it feels and what changes for you.

- Keep a journal to record your experiences. Write about moments when you acted according to your values and times when you drifted away from them. This helps you see your progress and adjust your path.

- Talk about your values with close friends or family. Sharing them can increase your commitment and help you understand how others see you. Sometimes, feedback is valuable in shaping your behavior.

- Maintaining Your Values Over Time

- Values can change or grow as you change. That's okay. Check in with yourself regularly to see if your values still fit the life you want. You might find that new experiences lead you to add or shift your values.

- Consistency is important, but so is flexibility. Being true to your values does not mean being rigid. It means choosing to act in ways that feel right for you. If you make a mistake, use it as a lesson. Forgive yourself and keep practicing living your values.

By living with clear values, you make your identity stronger and clearer. This makes everyday decisions easier and builds a life that feels real and meaningful.

Closing Reflection

Redefining your identity is a conscious act of liberation. You are not bound by old labels, roles, or expectations. You are allowed to evolve, shed what no longer fits, and consciously embrace the values that will guide your next chapter.

Step into this process with curiosity and compassion. Ask yourself:

- *Who do I want to be moving forward?*

- *What am I ready to release?*

- *What principles will guide me to my next step?*

Your identity is not fixed — it is alive, flexible, and waiting for your intentional creation. By redefining it, you reclaim the power to shape your life, detach from the past, and step fully into the person you are becoming.

Chapter 9
Embrace Uncertainty

S tarting over is inherently uncertain. You may not know exactly where you're going, what your life will look like, or how long it will take to feel settled. For many, this unknown feels frightening, even paralyzing. But uncertainty is not something to fear — it is the doorway to freedom, creativity, and growth. Learning to embrace it is one of the most powerful steps in detaching from the past and building a new life.

Starting Over Means Not Knowing — and That's Freedom

Understanding Our Need for Certainty

We all like to feel sure about what's coming next because it makes us feel safe. Certainty gives us a sense of control over our lives. When we know what to expect, we can plan and feel comfortable. For example, having a steady job or a predictable daily routine can make us feel secure. But the problem is, life doesn't always work that way. Things change, decisions come with risk, and outcomes are not guaranteed. When we cling too tightly to certainty, we might stay stuck in routines that do not make us happy anymore. We may hold onto relationships or habits simply because they feel familiar. Even if they don't bring us joy or growth, the comfort of certainty keeps us from making changes.

Letting Go to Start Fresh

Starting over means releasing the idea of what you thought your life should be. This can be hard because it feels like giving up on those plans and expectations. But starting over is also a chance to open up to new possibilities. It means letting go of the need to have all the answers. Imagine your life as a blank canvas. Not knowing what comes next is not a failure; it's an opportunity. You can begin to paint a new picture. This fresh start allows you to explore different paths, try new things, and find out what truly matters to you without being tied down by old ideas or pressures.

Changing How You Think About Failure and the Unknown

One way to make this shift is by changing your thoughts. Instead of saying, "*What if I fail?*" try asking yourself, "*What could I discover?*" This changes the focus from fear to curiosity. Fear of failure can hold us back from trying new things. But if you think about discovery, you open yourself to learning and growth, even if things do not go as planned. For example, if you decide to learn a new skill, like painting or coding, the worst that can happen is you don't get it immediately. But in the process, you may find new talents or interests you didn't know you had.

Similarly, instead of being afraid of the unknown, picture it as a field full of opportunities. When you don't know what comes next, it doesn't mean danger. It means new ideas, new people, and new directions that were hidden before. This mindset helps you see change as a chance to find paths that fit you better. Think of it like walking through a forest. You might not see the trail clearly at first, but as you keep moving, you discover new ways to go. Being open to the unknown invites adventure and learning.

Finding Freedom in Courage

Many believe that freedom comes when life feels certain and stable. But true freedom comes from having the courage to move forward even when you don't have all the answers. Taking steps into the unknown requires bravery. For example, if you want to switch careers, it might feel scary because you don't know if it will work out. But the choice to move anyway is what brings real freedom. It means you are not controlled by fear or comfort. Courage gives you the power to redefine your life and try new things. Even small steps, like reaching out to someone new or signing up for a class, build your confidence and open doors to freedom.

Practical Steps to Embrace Starting Over

To start letting go and embrace change, try small actions. First, write down your old expectations about your life. Look at them carefully and ask yourself if they still fit who you are now. Then, imagine what new goals or dreams you might have. Next, take a simple step toward those new ideas. It could be researching a new hobby, talking to people who inspire you, or planning a short trip to clear your mind. Notice how you feel when you move beyond old patterns. You might feel excited or nervous—that's normal. Keep reminding yourself that uncertainty is an open space for growth. Over time, these small steps will help you build a new path with more freedom and happiness.

Learn to Live in the "In-Between" With Curiosity

Life's Journey Is Not Straight or Simple

Life rarely follows a clear, straight path. When you face a big change, such as starting over, you enter what can be called the "in-between." This is the time or space between your old self and the new person you are becoming. It can feel strange or even uncomfortable because you lose the steady landmarks you once had. For example, if you changed careers, you might feel lost at first because you do not yet have clear goals or achievements in the new field. That feeling of being in-between is normal, but it's also very important. This space is where real change happens.

Many people want to rush through this awkward time to get to the "finished" version of their life. They want to know exactly where they are going and how things will turn out. But the truth is, change takes time. Instead of hurrying, it helps to slow down and be curious about the journey. When you enter this uncertain space, you can ask yourself helpful questions like, "What can I learn here?" These simple questions open doors to new insights, even in moments that seem confusing or difficult.

Practice Curiosity During Change

Curiosity means wanting to learn and discover new things. During times of change, it can be powerful to practice curiosity about your own experience. Instead of focusing on what you don't have or what you haven't achieved yet, pay attention to the small signs of progress around you. For example, if you are learning a new skill, notice the little improvements you make each day. Maybe you spent more time reading about the topic or tried a new approach. These small steps might seem minor, but they add up over time.

To stay curious, try to explore new interests and ideas without pressure. If you enjoy writing but don't know where it might lead, just write for the pleasure of it. If a new hobby catches your eye, give it a try without expecting to become an expert immediately. By exploring without a fixed goal, you allow yourself to grow naturally. This openness helps you stay connected to your true self and discover what really matters to you.

Turning Uncertainty into Opportunity

When you are in the in-between, it's normal to feel uncertain or even scared. You might worry about what the future holds or if you will succeed. But curiosity can help change how you think about uncertainty. Instead of seeing it as a problem, you can see it as an adventure. Think of uncertainty like an open road with many possibilities. This way of thinking encourages you to explore rather than avoid the unknown.

For example, if you just moved to a new city for work, instead of feeling lost, you might be curious about the new neighborhood. You could take walks to discover local shops, parks, or cafes. Trying new experiences, such as joining a club or taking a class, adds excitement and purpose. These actions turn fear of the unknown into chances for growth and learning.

Understanding the In-Between as a Growth Space

The in-between is not empty or pointless. It is fertile ground for building a new life that fits with your evolving self. When you think about growth, picture a seed planted in soil. At first, you cannot see much happening, but under the surface, roots are growing and getting stronger. The time you spend feeling uncertain or confused is like that underground work. Even if it doesn't feel productive, your mind and emotions are developing in important ways.

One way to use this in-between time wisely is to set simple daily or weekly intentions. For instance, you might decide to spend 15 minutes a day learning something new or reflecting on your feelings. You could keep a journal where you write about what you noticed during the day, what you tried, and what you felt. These small habits help you connect with your inner growth and recognize progress that is not always obvious.

Examples of Embracing the In-Between

There are many real-life stories of people who found strength in the in-between. Imagine someone who lost a job and didn't know what to do next. Instead of rushing to find another job of the same kind, they took time to explore their interests. They tried online courses, volunteered, or met new people in different fields. Through this curiosity, they discovered a passion for a career they had never thought about before. The in-between became a time of learning and discovery rather than fear and frustration.

Another example is a person going through a major life change like divorce or moving to a different country. The routines and plans they had were disrupted, and it felt like their life was on pause. However, by asking themselves what they could learn and trying new things, they slowly built a new, meaningful life. This time of uncertainty became the foundation for something better aligned with their values and dreams.

Steps to Make the Most of the In-Between

To make the most of this time, start by accepting that feeling lost or unsure is part of the process. Then, make a habit of asking yourself questions like, *"What did I learn today?"* or *"What small step can I take next?"* These questions help you focus on progress instead of perfection. It is also helpful to be gentle with yourself and allow time for mistakes and setbacks. Change is rarely smooth, and every experience, even failures, can teach you something useful.

Another step is to experiment with new activities or interests. For example, sign up for a workshop, join a local group, or start a small project. Pay attention to what excites you and what feels meaningful. If something does not feel right, that's okay too—it helps you narrow down what fits your new path. By staying open and curious, you create space for real growth.

Talking to others about your experience can also provide support and encouragement. Share your thoughts with friends, family, or a mentor. Sometimes, hearing different perspectives helps you see the possibilities more clearly. You might discover ideas or opportunities you hadn't considered before.

Final Thoughts on the In-Between

The in-between phase is not a failure or a pause—it is an important part of life's journey. It is where you learn, adapt, and grow into the person you are becoming. By practicing curiosity, noticing small progress, and exploring without pressure, you create a strong foundation for your future. Instead of rushing to the end, you can enjoy the process and find meaning along the way.

Treat Discomfort as a Sign of Growth, Not Danger

Understanding Uncertainty and Discomfort

Uncertainty is a feeling everyone experiences, and it usually makes us uncomfortable. When things are uncertain, you might notice feelings like anxiety, doubt, or even self-criticism popping up. These feelings happen naturally because our brains like knowing what's coming next. Not knowing can make us feel uneasy because it challenges our sense of control. However, feeling uncomfortable doesn't mean you are doing something wrong. Instead, it's a sign that you are growing or learning something new. For example, starting a new job often brings uncertainty and discomfort, but it also means you are stepping into a new role where you can build new skills and connections.

How Discomfort Signals Growth

Every time you face something unknown, whether it's making a difficult decision or trying a new skill, you are increasing your ability to bounce back from challenges—this ability is called resilience. You also become more creative because you have to think in new ways to solve problems. Courage grows too, because facing fear helps you see that you can handle more than you thought. Discomfort acts like a signal from your body and mind telling you that you are moving beyond what feels safe or familiar. Imagine trying to learn a new language. At first, it feels hard and uncomfortable because you are not used to the sounds or grammar rules. However, as you practice, your brain adapts, and you become better at understanding and speaking. This process shows how discomfort can mean you are breaking old patterns and expanding what you can do.

Reframing Discomfort When Fear Arises

When you feel fear or unease, it can help to change how you think about these feelings. Instead of seeing fear as a sign that you should stop, try telling yourself something positive. For example, you might say, "*I feel uncomfortable because I am stretching myself.*" This means you recognize that discomfort comes from pushing your limits in a good way. Another helpful thought is, "*This uncertainty is temporary, but the skills I'm developing are permanent.*" This reminder focuses on the fact that the difficult time will pass, but what you learn will stay with you for a long time. You can also think, "*Discomfort is the marker of progress, not failure.*" This means feeling uncomfortable is a way to see that you are making progress, not that you have done something wrong.

Embracing Discomfort as Part of Growth

When you accept that discomfort is natural and helpful, you start to see uncertainty differently. Instead of thinking of it as a roadblock, you begin to understand it as a partner on your journey. For instance, imagine training for a marathon. During the process, you will feel pain, tiredness, and frustration. These feelings are uncomfortable, but they are part of becoming a stronger runner. The same is true for personal growth. The more you face uncertainty and discomfort, the more you learn about yourself and what you can handle. This mindset helps you build freedom because you are not held back by fear. You recognize that moving forward often means stepping into the unknown, and that is okay. Over time, embracing discomfort can make you more confident in taking on new challenges.

Closing Reflection

Embracing uncertainty is not about pretending to be fearless. It's about choosing curiosity over avoidance, growth over comfort, and possibility over limitation.

Starting over will always involve the unknown. You may not know what comes next — and that is your greatest opportunity. Learn to live in the in-between, notice the lessons in discomfort, and trust that each step forward, even when it feels unstable, is part of the path to a new life.

Freedom lies not in certainty, but in your willingness to move forward anyway. Every time you face the unknown with courage, you detach further from the past and move closer to the life you are meant to create.

Chapter 10
Create New Routines & Rituals

T aking a new path in life can feel like stepping onto unfamiliar terrain. Everything feels new — exciting, yes, but also uncertain. In the midst of change, routines and rituals serve as anchors. They give your days structure, your mind a sense of order, and your life a rhythm you can rely on. Creating intentional routines doesn't restrict freedom; it provides a foundation for freedom to flourish.

Rituals Give Stability When Everything Else Feels New

Understanding Rituals and Their Role in Stability

When life feels uncertain and everything seems to be changing quickly, rituals can provide something steady to hold onto. A ritual is a practice that you do repeatedly and on purpose. It can be something simple or something with special meaning. What makes a ritual different from a habit is that it is done with intention and attention. You are aware of what you are doing and why you are doing it.

Rituals help your mind and body understand that even if many things are not stable, there are certain actions you can depend on. This feeling creates a sense of safety. When life feels chaotic, having something familiar can help you feel more in control. Rituals are like anchors, holding you in place when everything else moves around you.

What Makes a Ritual Different from a Habit

It is important to notice that not all repeated actions are rituals. For example, brushing your teeth is a habit because it is automatic and done without much thought. On the other hand, a ritual involves mindfulness, meaning you pay attention to the action and its meaning while you do it. You may do a ritual to set a mood, to calm yourself, or to prepare for something important. This purposeful focus adds value beyond the action itself.

A ritual does not have to be long or complicated. It can be a few seconds or several minutes. What matters is that you practice it regularly and find personal meaning in it. This connection to purpose helps your brain recognize it as something important, which builds a calming effect over time.

Examples of Simple Stabilizing Rituals

There are many kinds of rituals people create to help themselves when things around them feel unclear. For example, some might light a candle at the start of the day. Lighting a candle can become a symbol of beginning fresh and creating a peaceful space for work or study. The process of lighting the candle is a small action that signals your brain that it is time to focus.

Another routine could be brewing a cup of tea before starting work. The smell, the warmth of the cup, and the quiet moment to yourself all help slow your mind. The steps in this ritual can be: boiling water, choosing a tea bag, waiting for the tea to steep, and then taking a sip mindfully. This slows the pace, making the change from rest to work feel natural.

Going outside for a short walk in the morning is another example. This does not have to be a long exercise. Even five minutes of walking around the block can help. It gives you time to breathe fresh air, notice the sky or trees, and set your intentions quietly. You might decide that today you will focus on being kind, or simply remind yourself to take breaks. This ritual helps your mind start the day with a clear and calm focus.

Nighttime Rituals for Reflection and Release

Just as rituals can begin your day, they can also end your day. Many people find that journaling or meditating before bed helps them pause and reflect. To journal, you can write about what happened during the day, how you felt, and what you hope for tomorrow. You do not have to write many pages; even a few sentences help you connect with your thoughts.

Meditation is another way to reflect and release tension before sleeping. This can be as simple as sitting quietly for a few minutes, focusing on your breath, and letting go of the worries from the day. You might notice thoughts as they come and go, but not hold on to them. This helps clear your mind and prepare for rest.

Both journaling and meditating work as rituals by creating a boundary between the busy day and the quiet night. They tell your brain that it is time to stop working and relax, which can improve your sleep and help you feel calmer.

Building Rhythm and Consistency through Small Rituals

The key to rituals is practicing them often. Over time, small rituals add up. Doing them daily or several times a week helps create a steady rhythm in your life. This rhythm becomes familiar, and that familiarity supports you emotionally.

Starting new things or facing challenges can feel hard, but rituals make these moments easier. Because rituals are something repeatable and dependable, they provide a starting point. For example, if you have a ritual before work, like lighting a candle or making tea, it becomes a way to tell yourself, "*I am ready.*" This helps reduce hesitation or stress.

Rituals ground you in the present moment. When you focus on the simple steps of a ritual, your attention moves away from worries about the past or future. This mindfulness anchors you in now, which makes life feel more manageable.

How to Create Your Own Rituals

To create your own ritual, start by thinking about moments in your day when you need calm or focus. Choose something simple and meaningful. It could be a specific action like stretching, listening to a song, or even organizing your workspace.

Next, decide on the steps, which can be as few or as many as you want. Make sure the ritual fits easily into your routine so you can practice it regularly. For example, if you want a morning ritual, you can plan to brew tea and then spend five minutes reviewing your goals for the day.

Finally, be patient with yourself. It takes time for a ritual to become a part of your life. The more you do it intentionally, the stronger its effect will be. Keep in mind that rituals are personal. What works for one person might not work for another. Experiment and adjust your ritual until it feels right for you.

Start and End Your Day With Intention

Starting Your Day with Intention

How you start the morning can set the tone for the whole day. It doesn't have to be complicated or take a lot of time. One simple way to begin is by taking three deep breaths while you are still in bed. Deep breathing helps calm your nervous system and brings your attention to the present moment. For example, breathe slowly in through your nose for a count of four, hold for four, then breathe out through your mouth for a count of four. Doing this three times can help you wake up more peacefully and prepare your mind for the day ahead.

After calming your mind, writing down your top priorities can give your day structure. These priorities are not a full to-do list but the most important things you want to focus on. Pick no more than three. For instance, you might write "finish project report," "call Mom," and "go for a walk." Writing them down helps you stay focused and gives a sense of purpose, making it easier to manage your time. You could use a notebook, a planner app, or even sticky notes. The key is to make your priorities clear and visible.

Next, try saying a short affirmation or setting an intention that fits your goals or values. An affirmation is a positive statement that encourages your mindset. For example, you could say, "*I am confident and ready to face today*," or "*I choose kindness and patience*." If saying it out loud feels awkward, you can think it quietly or write it down. The idea is to align your mind with a positive direction. This small habit can boost your motivation and keep your thoughts focused throughout the day.

Ending Your Day with Intention

How you finish your day is just as important as how you start it. Taking a few moments before bedtime to reflect on what you accomplished can help you appreciate your efforts, no matter how big or small. These accomplishments might be simple things like replying to an email, cooking a healthy meal, or even making your bed. Recognizing these wins helps build confidence and creates a sense of progress. To do this, take a minute to write down or think about three things you did well today. This practice can encourage gratitude and a positive mindset before sleep.

Another important step in ending the day is releasing what you cannot control. Life often throws unexpected challenges, and holding onto stress or worry can make it hard to relax. You can try writing down your concerns and then imagining letting them go, like putting them in a box. You might say to yourself, "*I did my best, and I will handle what comes tomorrow.*" This process helps clear your mind and reduces anxiety. Practicing this regularly allows your mind to find peace and prepares you to rest better.

Preparing your space or mind for rest means creating an environment that invites relaxation. This might be tidying up your bedroom, dimming the lights, or turning off screens at least 30 minutes before bed. You could also try a simple calming activity, like reading a book, listening to soft music, or doing gentle stretches. For example, take a few minutes to gently stretch your arms and legs or to focus on your breathing while you sit quietly. These steps signal your body that it's time to slow down and recharge. Creating these habits makes falling asleep easier and improves the quality of your rest.

The Power of Rituals in Your Routine

By adding small, purposeful actions at the start and end of your day, you build routines that offer stability. These rituals become like bookends that frame your day, giving it structure and meaning. When life feels unpredictable, having these habits can reduce feelings of anxiety because your mind knows what to expect. This sense of continuity helps you feel more in control even when other things seem uncertain.

These rituals don't have to take long or require special tools. The key is consistency and making the habits fit your lifestyle. Over time, these simple actions can improve your focus during the day and help you relax at night. The benefits grow with regular practice, turning these small moments into a powerful support system for your mental health and daily productivity.

Replace Old Habits That Keep You Tied to Your Past

Letting Go of Old Habits

When you want to build new routines, one important step is to let go of old habits that keep you stuck in the past. Habits are like invisible strings that hold you back without you even realizing it. These habits create patterns that make it hard to change because they become automatic. To move ahead, it's important to first identify which habits no longer help you or support your goals. Once you know what they are, you can start to replace them with better ones that fit the new routines you want.

Recognizing the Habits That Don't Serve You

The first thing you need to do is look closely at your daily actions and notice which behaviors feel unhelpful. For example, maybe you spend a lot of time scrolling on your phone before bed, and this makes falling asleep harder. Or maybe you catch yourself thinking negative thoughts about yourself regularly. These are habits that make things harder for you. The goal is to spot these habits without judging yourself. This is a simple but important step to bring awareness to what you want to change.

Replace Instead of Remove

It might seem easy to just stop a bad habit, but if you simply remove it without putting something else in its place, you might find yourself slipping back into the old pattern. This is because when a habit stops, it creates a space that needs to be filled. If you leave that space empty, your mind or body tries to fill it with the familiar habit again. Instead, the best way to create lasting change is to consciously replace the old habit with a new one. This helps your brain build new connections and support the new lifestyle you want.

Practical Examples of Habit Replacement

One simple example is the habit of scrolling through social media while lying in bed. This might be your nightly routine, but it could interfere with your sleep or cause stress. To replace this, try keeping a book by your bedside. When you get into bed, pick up the book and read a few pages instead of grabbing your phone. Other good alternatives could be journaling about your day or stretching your body gently. These options not only keep your hands and mind busy but are also positive for calming your body and preparing for rest.

Changing Negative Self-Talk

Negative self-talk is a habit many people struggle with, and it can deeply affect your self-esteem and mood. Instead of simply trying to stop negative thoughts, replace them by practicing a daily affirmation or gratitude routine. For instance, each morning, say or write down a simple phrase like "I am capable" or "I am enough." If you want, add three things you are thankful for. Over time, this new practice can replace the old habit of critical thinking and help build a more positive mindset.

Being Mindful with Reactive Behaviors

Sometimes habits are about how we respond to situations, especially when we act without thinking. Impulsive or reactive behavior can lead to feelings of regret or stress. To replace this habit, introduce mindful pauses into your daily life. When you feel yourself reacting quickly, try to take a deep breath and count to three before responding. Reflection is key here. This brief pause gives you a moment to think about what's really going on and choose an action that is more thoughtful. Practicing this regularly will slowly change how you respond to triggers.

How to Make the New Habit Stick

Getting used to a new habit takes time and patience. One step to help the new habit grow is to link it to an existing routine. For instance, if you want to start reading at night, make it part of your bedtime routine after brushing your teeth. Small reminders, like putting a book on your pillow or writing an affirmation on a sticky note, help keep the new habit visible and easier to remember. When you do the new habit regularly, your brain starts to wire it in as the new normal.

The Role of Intentionality

Replacing habits is not something that happens by accident. It needs you to be intentional, which means you have to decide with care and focus to make the change. When you are intentional, you watch for moments when the old habit shows up and choose to step in with the new behavior instead. This also means accepting that you might slip back sometimes. When that happens, don't give up. Notice what caused the slip and use that information to strengthen your new habit next time.

<u>Summary of Steps to Replace Old Habits</u>

Here is a simple way to go about replacing habits:

- Identify the habit that no longer helps you.

- Understand what triggers the habit.

- Choose a new, positive habit that can fit the same trigger or situation.

- Make a clear plan for when and how you will practice the new habit.

- Use reminders and link the new habit to something old you already do.

- Be patient and consistent, allowing yourself to grow into the new habit.

- When you slip, review what happened and try again without judgment.

Building new routines by replacing old habits requires attention and care. When done well, it rewires your behaviors and sets you on a path to the life you want to live.

Closing Reflection

New routines and rituals are the scaffolding for your fresh start. They provide stability when everything feels new, set intention at the beginning and end of your days, and replace patterns that tie you to the past.

Starting over is not about rushing forward recklessly. It's about moving deliberately, step by step, anchored by practices that support your growth. Every morning and evening, every small ritual, reinforces the life you're choosing to create — a life aligned with your intentions, free from the weight of old habits, and guided by the new story you are writing.

Part V
Renewal
Moving Forward with
Meaning & Peace

Chapter 11

Surround Yourself with Growth Energy

W hen you're rebuilding your life, the energy around you matters as much as the effort within you. Who and what you allow into your space influences your mindset, your confidence, and your ability to keep moving forward.

Starting over is not just about changing what you *do* — it's also about changing what you *absorb*. The people you spend time with, the conversations you engage in, and the content you consume all feed your inner world.

To grow, you must curate your surroundings with intention — choosing energy that uplifts, not drains.

Spend Time With People Who Inspire Progress

Finding the Right People When You're Starting Over

Starting over can be tough. It might feel like you're stepping into the unknown, unsure of what will happen next. During these times, the people you spend time with are very important. You want to be around people who see your potential. These are the ones who believe you can grow and improve, instead of focusing on what you can't do. They won't hold you back or make you feel small. Instead, they push you to rise up and try new things.

People who focus on growth don't always have perfect lives. They still face problems, struggles, and setbacks. But what makes them different is the way they think about these struggles. They look forward and believe in the power of effort, not just talent. They know that being resilient—getting up after falling—is a key part of life. They also understand that growth comes bit by bit. Even small steps count towards becoming better.

How Growth-Oriented People Help You

When you start something new, like a new job, hobby, or way of living, you will probably doubt yourself sometimes. This is normal. It can be very helpful to have people around who encourage you during those moments. Growth-oriented friends or mentors will remind you that feeling doubt is just part of learning. They cheer you on and give you support when you feel unsure.

These people also remind you of your progress, especially at times when you don't see it yourself. Sometimes, you may feel stuck or like you are not moving forward. But someone who cares about your growth can point out the small progress you did make. For example, if you learned a new skill or handled a difficult situation better than before, they will notice it and celebrate it with you. This helps you stay motivated and confident.

Celebrating small wins is very important on the journey of starting over. Growth-oriented people understand how hard it can be to reach even little goals. They don't wait until big successes to celebrate. Instead, they celebrate every small step you take, whether it's finishing a task, learning something new, or simply showing up each day. This kind of support helps you see your efforts as valuable.

The Power of an Intentional Circle

When you're starting over, you might think you need a lot of friends or a big social circle. But that's not true. What really matters is having a small, intentional group of people around you. Intentional means these people are not random or just around by chance. They are the ones you choose because they support who you want to become.

Surrounding yourself with people who match your goals and values helps you grow in the right ways. They should reflect the person you are becoming, not just the person you used to be. For example, if you want to be more honest, creative, and alive, spend time with people who already value these things. That way, their habits and ways of thinking will influence you.

Choosing People Who Inspire Honesty and Creativity

Being honest with yourself and others takes courage. Not everyone encourages you to be open about your feelings or thoughts. But growth-oriented people create a safe space where you can express yourself honestly without judgment. This makes it easier to face challenges and learn from mistakes.

Creativity is another quality that growth-focused people nurture. When you try new ways of solving problems or express yourself in different ways, it helps you grow. For example, friends who share new ideas, encourage experimentation, or support creative projects can spark your own creativity. They make you feel excited about what you can make or discover.

Being Around People Who Help You Feel More Alive

Feeling alive means feeling fully present and engaged in your life. Sometimes, starting over can make you feel tired or disconnected. But spending time with people who bring energy and positivity can change that. They help you see life as an adventure instead of a set of problems.

These people might motivate you to try new things, laugh more, or step outside your comfort zone. For example, they might invite you to take a walk, try a new hobby, or simply share stories that make you feel connected. Being with them helps you feel more joy and excitement about your life.

How to Find These People

Finding the right people isn't always easy, especially if you're starting fresh. One way is to look for groups or communities that share your interests or values. For example, if you want to learn painting, join a local art class or online group. There, you can meet people who also want to grow creatively.

Another way is to reach out to mentors or role models you respect. They can offer advice and encouragement based on their own experiences. Even if you don't know them personally, reading their books or listening to their talks can help you develop a growth mindset.

Also, pay attention to the people you already know. Some old friends or colleagues might be growth-oriented, even if you didn't see it before. Try spending more time with those who inspire and support you, and less time with those who bring doubt or negativity.

How to Keep Your Circle Intentional

Once you find people who positively influence you, nurture those relationships. Make time to talk with them regularly, share your thoughts and listen to theirs. Show appreciation for their support. This builds trust and deepens the connection.

At the same time, it's okay to set boundaries with people who don't support your growth. You don't have to cut them out completely, but limit the impact they have on your mindset. Remember, you're choosing who helps you grow, not who drags you down.

The Long-Term Impact

Over time, an intentional circle of growth-oriented people shapes your behavior, thinking, and feelings. Their encouragement helps you build confidence. Their reminders keep you moving forward. Their celebrations make the journey enjoyable.

When you surround yourself with the right people, you create an environment where change and growth are possible. You are not alone. Together, you work towards becoming the person you want to be, step by step.

Remember: inspiration is contagious — but so is stagnation. Choose accordingly.

Distance Yourself From Constant Negativity

Understanding the Need for Boundaries When Starting Over

When you decide to start over in life, not everyone will understand or support your choice. People around you may react in ways that seem negative or unsupportive. Some might project their own fears, doubts, or bitterness onto you. This doesn't necessarily mean these people are bad or mean, but it does mean you need to set boundaries. Boundaries are limits you put in place to protect your emotional and mental well-being. They help you avoid getting pulled into negativity that can slow down your progress.

For example, if a friend always tells you that trying something new won't work because they failed, that is their fear, not your reality. It's helpful to recognize this and set a boundary by gently telling them that you appreciate their concern but want to focus on your own path. Setting boundaries can feel awkward at first, but it's an important step to protect your motivation.

The Impact of Constant Negativity

Negativity can come from many places: relationships with family and friends, your job, or even places you visit online. When you are surrounded by constant negativity, it can drain your energy and cloud your mind. This makes it hard to stay motivated or to think clearly about your goals and dreams. You might find yourself stuck in old stories about failure or limits that no longer serve you.

For instance, if your workplace is filled with people who complain about everything or don't support new ideas, it can be hard to stay excited about your work or your future. The energy around you shapes how you feel inside. It's like being in soil that has too many weeds — it's difficult for new plants to grow. Recognizing this is the first step in deciding to change your environment or how you interact with it.

Why Protecting Your Peace is Wise, Not Unkind

Sometimes, stepping back from people or situations that make you feel bad is seen as rude or unkind. But protecting your peace means taking care of yourself. It's a wise choice, not a selfish one. Your peace is your mental calm and emotional balance. When you protect it, you create space for growth and healing.

Imagine that your peace is like a clear glass of water. If it gets dirty with negativity or stress, it becomes hard to see through or feel calm. Protecting your peace might mean saying no to extra work when you feel overwhelmed, or leaving a party early if conversations make you anxious. These actions help keep your inner balance and make sure you have energy for what matters most.

Questions to Help You Identify What to Change

To figure out where to put boundaries or distance yourself, it helps to ask some simple questions. One question is: who leaves me feeling tired or drained after I spend time with them? This helps identify people who may be negative or demanding, even if they don't mean to be. Another question is: who genuinely supports me to grow without judging or competing with me? These are the people who encourage you and want the best for you.

You can also ask yourself where you can create more emotional distance without feeling guilty. Emotional distance means not getting too involved in drama or negative conversations, and it's okay to do this. You do not owe anyone your emotional energy all the time, especially if it harms your well-being.

Different Ways to Create Distance

Creating distance doesn't always mean ending relationships or making big changes. Sometimes, it can be simple actions like spending less time with certain people or avoiding tricky topics in conversations. For example, if a friend always talks negatively about your goals, you might change the subject when it comes up or suggest talking about something else. This allows you to keep the friendship but protect your own energy.

Another way to create distance is to limit the time you spend in places that feel toxic. This could mean leaving a social media group that is full of complaints or reducing hours at a job that doesn't support you. These steps don't have to be dramatic but adding small adjustments can make a big difference in how you feel.

Growing in Healthy Environments

You can't grow or feel good when your surroundings are full of negativity. Think about planting a garden. If the soil is poisoned, plants won't thrive no matter how much you water them or how much sunlight they get. Your environment, including the people and places around you, is like the soil. It influences your growth and happiness.

If you find that your current "soil" is full of negativity, give yourself permission to find new places or people to support you. This can mean spending more time with friends who lift you up or joining new groups that share your interests. It can also mean learning new skills or finding hobbies that make you feel joyful and energized.

Planting elsewhere means making conscious choices about where you spend your time and energy. It is about creating a life that supports your dreams and helps you become who you want to be. This might mean trying new things, meeting new people, or simply focusing on yourself for a while. Whatever it looks like for you, choosing a healthy environment is important for your success and peace of mind.

Follow Content That Feeds Your Goals, Not Your Fear

The Influence of Digital Content on Your Life

In today's world, the things you consume online are just as important as the people you spend time with. Everything you see or hear on social media, podcasts, the news, or even TV shows helps shape your thoughts and feelings. This digital content affects how you think about yourself and the world around you. It can build you up or tear you down. So, it's important to think carefully about what you let into your mind through your digital channels.

Being Careful with Your Digital Diet

When you are rebuilding your life, the things you watch, read, or listen to become even more important. It's like choosing the food you eat — you want to nourish your mind, not fill it with junk. A helpful question to ask yourself is: "Does this content inspire me to take action, or does it make me feel stuck or scared?" If something makes you feel too afraid or hopeless, it's probably not good for you right now. Instead, try to focus on digital material that helps you move forward and grow.

Following Content That Supports Your Goals

One way to do this is by following creators who share real wisdom and progress. These people offer practical tools that you can use in your life to improve yourself. For example, their advice might include daily habits to stay focused, ways to manage your time better, or tips to build confidence. Follow these creators on social media or subscribe to their channels so you get regular reminders to keep growing.

Listening to Stories of Resilience

Another helpful habit is to listen to stories about resilience. Resilience means the ability to keep going even when things are tough. Unlike the drama-filled content that cycles around problems without solutions, stories of resilience show how people overcome hardships. For example, a podcast might feature someone who lost their job but found a new career by learning new skills. Hearing these stories can give you hope and ideas for your own life.

Reading to Expand Your Mind

Reading books or articles is a great way to grow your mind. But it's important to pick material that broadens your thinking. Avoid things that only repeat the same narrow views or make you feel trapped in your current mindset. Instead, choose books or articles that offer new ideas, explain different points of view, or teach skills relevant to your goals. For example, if you are trying to be more confident, you might read a self-help book that explains simple techniques like positive affirmations or goal setting.

Protecting Your Attention as a Valuable Resource

Your attention is very valuable. Think of it like a limited resource that should be spent wisely. When you feed your attention with positive and helpful content, you reinforce the new path you are on. But if you spend time on things that pull you back into old habits, negativity, or fear, your progress will slow down. So, it's important to be mindful about what you pay attention to. For example, if you notice that scrolling through social media leaves you feeling anxious or unsuccessful, try setting limits on your screen time or unfollowing accounts that bring you down.

Taking Simple Steps to Curate Your Digital Space

Start by making a list of digital content that makes you feel good and motivates you. Then, look at who you follow on social media and decide if they fit that list. If not, don't hesitate to unfollow or mute those accounts. Try subscribing to a few podcasts that focus on personal development or success stories. Make a habit of reading one helpful article or a chapter from a good book each day. Over time, these small steps will create a digital environment that supports your growth and rebuilding process.

Managing Digital Overload with Attention Controls

It's easy to feel overwhelmed by the vast amount of content online. To manage this, use tools like apps that track your screen time or set daily limits on how long you spend on certain sites. For example, many phones have built-in features that allow you to see your usage and set reminders to take breaks. This helps you avoid falling into the trap of endless scrolling, which often leads to feeling stuck or unhappy. Instead, these controls help keep your mind clear and focused on what really matters.

Creating a Routine Focused on Growth

Try to create a daily routine that includes time for consuming inspiring digital content. For instance, you can start your morning by listening to a motivational podcast or reading a chapter from a self-improvement book. This sets a positive tone for the day. In the evening, avoid watching the news or social media if you find that it makes you anxious or tired. Instead, perhaps watch a documentary that teaches you something new or read a story about someone who turned their life around.

Benefits of a Positive Digital Diet

When you focus your digital diet on helpful and inspiring content, you'll likely notice changes. You may feel more motivated to take action. You might start trying new habits or facing challenges with less fear. Your mind becomes more open to growth and new opportunities. Plus, by avoiding content that causes comparison, anger, or despair, you protect your mental health. This helps you build a stronger foundation for the new life you want to create.

Closing Reflection

Starting over requires courage — but staying the course requires *energy*. The company you keep, the conversations you engage in, and the content you consume all shape the emotional fuel that powers your journey.

Surround yourself with people who inspire progress, not paralysis. Step back from negativity without apology. Feed your mind with content that aligns with your goals and values.

You are not obligated to remain in environments that drain you. By choosing growth energy — in your relationships, habits, and digital world — you're not just protecting your peace; you're nurturing the life you're creating.

This is how momentum builds: one conversation, one boundary, one conscious choice at a time.

Chapter 12
Take Aligned Action

There comes a point in every new beginning where thinking, planning, and preparing aren't enough — you have to *move*.

Starting your life over means stepping into action, even when you're not sure how it will unfold. The truth is, clarity doesn't come before action; it comes *because* of it.

You can't build a new life by staying in your head. You build it by showing up in small, deliberate ways that match the person you're becoming. That's what aligned action is — movement guided by intention, not fear.

Stop Overthinking and Do One Thing That Moves You Forward

Understanding Overthinking and Preparation

Overthinking often feels like it's part of getting ready for something important. You might tell yourself that you need to plan a bit more or find another sign before starting. Maybe you think you need one more tip or piece of advice to feel sure. The problem is, this overthinking can stop you from moving forward. It tricks you into waiting for the perfect moment, when really, you already know what your next small step should be. Recognizing this is the first step to breaking free from getting stuck in your head.

The Courage to Take One Step

What you really need isn't a perfect plan or the whole map laid out in front of you. What you need is the courage to take one step in the right direction. Think of your journey like walking out the door on a foggy morning. You don't see the whole path clearly, but you trust that moving forward is better than standing still. That one small step could be as simple as sending a message or setting a timer to start working. The important part is to move, even just a little. This movement creates momentum that will carry you along.

Questions to Help You Move Forward

When you feel stuck, it helps to ask yourself some simple questions. These questions focus your attention on what you can do right now, instead of worrying about everything all at once. For example, ask yourself, "*What's one action I can take today that supports my new path?*" This means choosing one thing that moves you closer to your goal. It could be something small like researching options or writing a draft. The key is to choose something manageable so you don't feel overwhelmed.

Another useful question is, "*What's one thing I've been putting off because I'm afraid it won't be perfect?*" Often, fear of making mistakes or not doing something perfectly can stop us from even starting. By identifying one task you've delayed for this reason, you can focus your energy on pushing through that fear. Just doing one imperfect thing is better than waiting for everything to be perfect.

Taking Action, Even When It's Small

Once you decide on the one small action, take it. It might feel scary or uncomfortable, but that's okay. The size of the step doesn't matter as much as actually moving forward. For example, if you want to make a change in your career, you could send an email to ask about a course or a job opening. If you want to write a book, try writing the first page without worrying about how good it sounds. If you want to get healthier, just go for a short walk around the block. These small actions add up over time.

Doing something "messy" means you don't wait for everything to be perfect before starting. Perfectionism can paralyze progress, making it worse than taking a step that's a little rough around the edges. This is how you build confidence and keep your momentum going.

Examples of Small but Important Steps

Here are some examples of what you might do to start moving forward:

- Send that email you've been avoiding. It could be to a mentor, a potential client, or a school. The act of reaching out often makes a big difference.

- Make the call that seems hard. A phone call can be more personal and effective than email, and it moves the process forward quickly.

- Write the first page of something you want to create — a story, a report, a blog post. Don't worry about editing it yet.

- Take a walk to clear your mind and get your body moving. This simple step can help your brain work better and reduce stress.

- Apply for a class or program you've been interested in. Even if you're unsure or nervous, applying is a way of committing to your goal.

Momentum Starts with Movement

One of the most important ideas to remember is that momentum does not come from having all the answers or knowing exactly what to do next. Momentum begins with movement, no matter how small or imperfect. The act of doing something—anything that moves you closer to your aim—builds energy and confidence. It helps reduce the pressure of trying to figure everything out at once.

You don't need to have a full plan or be ready for every possible situation before you start. Waiting for the right moment or a perfect plan can keep you stuck for a long time. Instead, try to focus on what you can do right now. This mindset helps you to break projects down into manageable pieces and prevents feeling overwhelmed. It leads to progress.

Starting Without Having It All Figured Out

It can be tempting to put off starting until you feel completely ready. You might want to have a full schedule, all your materials, or a perfect outline. But this kind of thinking often stops people from ever beginning at all. The truth is, you don't need to have everything figured out to get started. Just beginning, even with something tiny, is enough to create the change you want.

Beginning can mean different things to different people. It might be writing a short list of priorities, making an appointment, or researching a topic for 10 minutes. It doesn't have to be a big leap – any forward motion counts. By focusing on starting, you take control over your own progress instead of waiting for external factors to line up. This simple shift can make a huge difference in reaching your goals.

Build Momentum Through Consistency, Not Intensity

Starting Over: The Temptation of Fast Results

When you decide to start over, it's natural to want to see quick changes. You might find yourself eager to make a lot of progress right away. This often means setting big goals, trying out new habits all at once, or completely changing your daily routine. For example, someone might decide to wake up two hours earlier, start exercising for an hour every day, change their diet, and take a new course—all in the same week. This kind of quick, intense effort feels encouraging at first because it shows you are committed to change. However, this burst of energy can be hard to keep up. After a few days or weeks, the initial excitement can fade. When that happens, you might feel tired, overwhelmed, or even disappointed with yourself for not keeping up. This leads to burnout, where you give up the new habits and go back to old patterns.

Why Consistency Matters More Than Intensity

Real, lasting progress happens through consistency. Consistency means doing a little bit regularly, not all at once. When you show up every day to work on your goals, even if it's just a small effort, you build trust with yourself. Trusting yourself means you believe you can follow through on your promises. For example, if you decide to read 10 pages of a book every day and actually do it, you prove to yourself that you arc reliable. This trust makes it easier to keep going because you feel more confident. It's not necessary to make huge changes overnight. Instead, slow and steady steps that match the new path you want to take are much more effective.

The Power of Small Daily Actions

Doing a little bit each day is much better than doing a lot one day and nothing for the next several days. Small actions, repeated often, add up over time. This is called compound growth. Imagine saving one dollar every day. After a year, you'll have saved 365 dollars. That's much more than saving ten dollars one day and zero the rest of the year. The same goes for habits and personal growth. If you practice a skill for 10 minutes daily, you will improve more than practicing for an hour once a week. Also, the key is not to aim for perfect actions every time. It's okay if some days you do things imperfectly or less than usual. What matters most is showing up regularly. You can think of this as planting seeds every day: some days you water your plants thoroughly, other days just a little, but you keep taking care of them. Over time, these daily efforts lead to growth and change.

Aligned Action Is Like a Heartbeat

Aligned action means doing things that match your goals and your new direction in life. It's important to think of this action not as a sprint but as a steady beat—like a heartbeat. A heartbeat is steady, rhythmic, and ongoing. It keeps going without stopping, which supports life. When your efforts are steady like this, they keep your progress alive and growing. Instead of trying to make huge, fast changes that can stop suddenly, focus on keeping consistent, reasonable energy. For instance, if you want to become healthier, instead of doing a long workout once a week, try to move a little every day, like taking a walk, stretching, or doing a quick home exercise. This way, you maintain momentum and the change starts to feel natural. Over time, your new habits settle in and become part of who you are.

Practical Steps to Build Consistency

If you want to build consistency, start with small, manageable goals that you can do every day. For example, if you want to read more, start with just five minutes a day. Set a reminder on your phone or attach this habit to something you already do, like reading right after breakfast. Track your progress in a simple journal or app, so you can see how many days in a row you have completed your small task. This helps you stay motivated.

If you miss a day, don't give up. Just start again the next day. Remember, it's better to do a little than nothing at all.

Another helpful step is to prepare your environment to support your new habits. For example, if you want to eat healthier, keep fruits and vegetables visible and easy to grab in your kitchen. Remove or hide unhealthy snacks. This makes it easier to follow through without relying only on willpower. Think about what might get in your way and plan simple solutions. Having a friend or family member join you or check in on progress can also help keep you accountable and consistent.

Understanding Motivation and Discipline

Motivation often comes and goes. You might feel excited to change one day, but the next day, not so much. This is normal. Because motivation is unpredictable, it's not a good foundation for lasting change. Instead, discipline becomes crucial. Discipline means doing what you need to do, even when you don't feel like it. Building discipline takes time and practice. One way to do this is by creating routines. For instance, if you want to start writing, set a rule to write for at least 10 minutes at the same time every day. Following a routine makes the action automatic; you don't have to rely on motivation to get started. Over time, the routine feels natural and the discipline becomes stronger.

Seeing Progress Over Time

When you focus on consistency, it might feel like you are not making big progress because each step is small. However, change often happens slowly. Think about how muscles grow after regular exercise or how language improves after daily practice. The results come little by little until one day they become obvious. It helps to find ways to notice these small wins. For example, if your goal is to get fit, instead of only looking at your weight, notice how your clothes fit or how much energy you have during the day. Celebrate these small signs of progress. This keeps you encouraged and reminds you why the consistent effort is worth it.

Building Patience and Realistic Expectations

Starting over means accepting that change is a process. It rarely happens instantly or perfectly. Expecting fast transformation puts a lot of pressure on yourself and can set you up for disappointment. Being patient means giving yourself time to learn, adjust, and grow. Understand that setbacks and slow days are part of the journey, not reasons to stop. If you set realistic expectations and focus on steady progress, you can avoid frustration. For example, if you want to learn guitar, recognize that you won't play perfect songs in a few weeks. Instead, enjoy each small improvement and practice regularly. This mindset helps you stay calm and keep going.

Summary of Key Ideas

Starting over is exciting, but bursts of intense effort usually don't last. Consistency is the key to real progress, showing you can rely on yourself with small, steady actions. These small steps add up over time to create real change. Think of your progress like a heartbeat, something steady and ongoing. Use simple habits, set small goals, and prepare your environment to support your new routines. Understand that motivation will vary, so discipline and routine are your tools for success. Watch for small signs of growth and be patient with the process. Change takes time, but consistent effort will get you there.

Action Brings Clarity Faster Than Reflection Alone

Reflection and Its Importance

Reflection means thinking deeply about your experiences, choices, and feelings. It is a valuable process because it helps you understand what has happened and why. When you take time to reflect, you can learn from your past actions and experiences. For example, after finishing a project, you might sit down and ask yourself what went well and what did not. This helps you recognize patterns that you might want to keep or change in the future. Reflection also helps you make better plans because it lets you see what worked and what didn't. However, reflection alone doesn't solve all problems or lead you to success.

The Limits of Reflection Without Action

While reflection is useful, it can also become a way to avoid doing things. Sometimes people spend a lot of time thinking, journaling, or reading, hoping to find the perfect answer. Yet, no matter how much you reflect or gather information, you won't really know what works for you until you try things out in real life. For example, you might spend months writing in a journal about your career goals and reading books about success, but this won't give you the real experience of working in different jobs or industries. Reflection without action can become a type of safe zone where you feel busy but don't make real progress.

Action as a Feedback Loop

Taking action is essential because it creates a feedback loop. This means when you do something, you get information in return. Each step you take teaches you something new about yourself and your surroundings. For example, if you start a new hobby like painting, after a few sessions you will notice what excites you about it and what parts feel boring or frustrating. This feedback helps you make better choices next time. You learn what energizes you and what drains your energy, helping you focus on activities that bring joy and success. Action helps you discover the direction that feels right for you, whether it's in your personal life, career, or relationships.

Learning What Energizes You

When you act, you begin to understand what things give you energy and make you feel good. This might be a task, a topic, or a type of people you interact with. For example, if you try volunteering at different organizations, you might find that working with children is exciting and fulfilling, but organizing events feels tiring and stressful. Recognizing what energizes you is important because it helps you choose paths that keep you motivated and happy. You can take steps such as making a list of activities you have tried recently and rating how much energy they gave you afterward. This clear record can guide your future decisions.

Seeing What Drains You

Just as action helps you find what energizes you, it also reveals what drains your energy. These are activities or situations that leave you feeling tired, frustrated, or burned out. For example, you might discover that working long hours without breaks or being in competitive environments makes you feel stressed and unhappy. Knowing these details helps you avoid or change these energy-draining situations. You can take simple actions to protect your energy, such as setting boundaries with work hours or limiting time spent on stressful tasks. Over time, these adjustments improve your well-being and productivity.

Discovering What Direction Feels Right

Eventually, by trying different things and paying attention to the feedback from your actions, you start to find a direction that feels right for you. This direction is a combination of what you enjoy, what you are good at, and what fits your values. For example, someone might try different jobs, hobbies, or volunteering roles, and through the process, realize that helping others is what brings them fulfillment. You don't discover this direction by only thinking about it; it emerges from actual experience. Small steps like joining clubs, attending workshops, or taking short courses can help you explore different paths until you find one that suits you.

Readiness Comes from Doing

Many people wait to "feel ready" before starting something new. They want to have everything planned perfectly or to be sure of success before they take the first step. The truth is readiness does not come before you start; it is something you earn by acting. For example, you might want to learn a new language but delay starting because you don't feel prepared. Starting with simple exercises or basic conversations builds your confidence and skills over time. Readiness grows as you move forward and gain experience, not while you sit waiting. Taking small, manageable actions can build the readiness you need for bigger challenges.

Moving Forward Through Experimentation

The best way to find out what works for you is to move forward by experimenting. Trying different things allows you to gather useful information. For example, if you want to improve your health, experiment with different diets and exercises. Notice how your body feels with each change. Pay attention to energy levels, mood, and strength. Based on your observations, you can adjust your plan. This trial-and-error approach helps you create a way of living that fits your unique needs. Always be open to change and ready to try new methods rather than sticking to one plan that doesn't feel right.

Adjusting Based on Experience

When you take action and experiment, you will sometimes find that things don't go as you expected. This is a normal part of the process. Adjusting means making changes based on what you learn from your actions. For example, if you start a job and realize the hours or tasks aren't a good fit, you can look for ways to change your schedule or find new roles that suit you better. Adjustment keeps you flexible and moving forward. It is like steering a ship; you correct your direction depending on the wind and waves until you reach your destination. Small adjustments help you stay on track toward what feels right.

Clarity Comes from Doing, Not Overthinking

Overthinking can make decisions harder and slow you down. It can create confusion because you get stuck looking at every possible option without actually moving forward. Clarity is not about having all the answers before you begin. It comes from doing, experimenting, and learning along the way. For example, writing a story may seem overwhelming if you spend too long planning every detail. Writing the first draft quickly and then revising it many times often leads to clearer and better results. Each action, no matter how small, gives you more understanding than hours spent thinking without action.

Closing Reflection

Taking aligned action is about more than productivity — it's about integrity. It's about aligning what you *want* with what you *do*.

Stop waiting for perfect conditions. Stop assuming clarity must come before movement. Life rewards direction, not hesitation.

Take one small, purposeful action that moves you toward your new beginning. Do it again tomorrow. Keep showing up, even when it's uncertain.

Each step will reveal the next one.
Each act of courage will strengthen your trust in yourself.
And before you know it, you won't just be starting over — you'll be building something that feels deeply, powerfully aligned with who you've become.

Chapter 13
Find Meaning in the Mess

When life falls apart, it's natural to want to move on as quickly as possible — to sweep away the chaos, silence the pain, and get back to "normal." But starting over isn't just about moving forward; it's about *understanding* what your past was trying to teach you.

The mess, as uncomfortable as it is, holds meaning. It's the raw material for your next chapter — a source of insight, compassion, and strength that no easy season could ever give you.

Finding meaning in the mess doesn't mean pretending pain was good. It means allowing it to shape you, not shatter you.

Pain Can Be a Teacher, Not Just a Setback

Understanding Pain and Its Role in Our Lives

Pain often feels like a punishment, especially when it catches us off guard or when we believe we don't deserve it. At those moments, it is easy to question why life is being so hard on us. However, pain has a different role than just causing suffering. It can reveal important truths that comfort often hides. For example, when you are physically hurt, pain signals to you that something is wrong and needs attention. Similarly, emotional pain alerts us to areas in our lives that need change or healing. This shift in perspective helps us see pain not just as a negative experience, but as a kind of message or guide.

Pain helps us identify what really matters in our lives. When everything feels fine, we might take many things for granted. But during hard times, we start to notice what is truly important — it could be our relationships, our health, or even our sense of self. For instance, if you lose a job unexpectedly, the pain of that loss might make you realize you were not happy in your previous role. This realization can push you to search for better opportunities that fit what you truly value. Pain also teaches us what we need to let go of. Holding on to certain habits, thoughts, or relationships might have been possible when life was easier, but pain can reveal that these things are no longer helpful or healthy. Letting go is never simple, but pain can motivate this difficult step.

Lessons From Life's Hardest Moments

When you look back on the toughest times you have faced, you might notice that these moments taught you important lessons. One such lesson is about resilience. Resilience is the ability to bounce back after difficulties. For example, someone who has experienced failure might learn how to keep trying, even after being disappointed. This quality is not usually something that develops when life is smooth. It is earned during moments of struggle. If you reflect on a hard experience, try to ask yourself how you managed to keep going. Maybe you found support from friends or family, or maybe you discovered inner strength you didn't know you had.

Hard moments also teach us about boundaries. Boundaries are the limits we set in our relationships and lives to protect our well-being. Pain can show us when these boundaries have been crossed. For example, if a friendship consistently causes you stress or sadness, the pain you feel might be signaling that you need to take a step back. Learning to say no, or to distance yourself from harmful situations, is a skill that often grows out of experience with pain. Another important insight we gain from difficult times is about who we really are when everything familiar disappears. Sometimes, we build our identity around certain roles, habits, or comforts. When these things are taken away, we have the chance to discover a deeper part of ourselves.

Changing the Question: From "Why Me?" to "What Can I Learn?"

One of the biggest changes you can make in dealing with pain is the way you ask questions about it. Many people naturally ask, "*Why did this happen to me?*" This question focuses on blame and suffering, which can leave you feeling stuck and powerless. On the other hand, asking, "*What can this teach me?*" shifts the focus to learning and growth. This shift helps reclaim your power over the situation.

For instance, if you have a break-up, instead of dwelling on the unfairness of it, you can ask what lessons the experience offers. You might learn more about what you want in a partner, or how to communicate better next time. This mindset does not mean ignoring the pain. Instead, it invites you to use the pain as a tool for personal development. Over time, pain becomes less of a thief that takes away your happiness and more of a teacher that helps you grow stronger and wiser.

Growth Happens in Discomfort

Growth is rarely easy. It usually occurs when we are uncomfortable — when situations force us to face parts of ourselves or our lives that need change. Imagine a plant growing towards the sunlight. To do so, it must push through the soil. Similarly, personal growth requires facing challenges and discomfort.

If you want to learn from pain, start by being open to what it shows you. Take time to reflect on your experiences, journal your thoughts, or talk to someone you trust. For example, if you are dealing with the pain of failure, write down what went wrong and what you could do differently next time. This process helps transform the discomfort into practical steps toward improvement. Avoid rushing to escape the pain. Instead, lean into it a little and allow it to guide your next actions.

When pain reveals a part of your life that needs transformation, take small, clear steps to make changes. If the pain comes from poor health, you might start by scheduling a check-up, adjusting your diet, or beginning a simple exercise routine. If the pain is emotional, such as feeling lonely, consider reaching out to friends, joining a group activity, or seeking therapy. Growth is a gradual process, and each small action builds momentum.

Let Pain Educate, Not Define

It is important to remember that pain does not have to define who you are. Many people carry hard experiences with them, but instead of letting those experiences control their lives, they use them to learn and grow. For example, a person who survived a serious illness might choose to use that pain to inspire healthier choices and gratefulness, rather than letting the experience cause lasting fear or bitterness.

Accepting pain as part of life allows us to live more fully. When you let pain educate you, it becomes a source of knowledge and strength. Keep in mind that pain is temporary, while what you learn from it can last a lifetime. Taking the lessons from pain will help you move forward with more wisdom, better boundaries, and a clearer sense of who you are.

Ask What This Chapter in Your Life Is Trying to Show You

Every Chapter in Your Life Has a Message

Life is made up of many chapters, just like a book. Each chapter tells part of your story. Some chapters are happy, and some are painful. Even the painful parts have something important to teach you. The hard times can feel overwhelming, but if you learn to listen carefully, you will find they carry messages that can help you grow.

Listening to life's messages means paying attention to your experiences and what they show you. Instead of ignoring or avoiding difficult moments, try to reflect on them. Ask yourself what you can learn. For example, after a tough breakup, you might realize you need clearer boundaries in relationships. Or after a failure at work, you might discover new strengths you didn't know you had. This kind of thinking helps you turn pain into something useful.

What Patterns are You Being Invited to Break?

One important question to ask yourself is what patterns keep showing up in your life. Patterns are habits or ways of acting that happen again and again. Sometimes these patterns cause problems or keep you stuck. For example, maybe you often choose friends who don't treat you well or take on too much responsibility and burn out. When pain or difficulty repeats, it is a signal to notice those patterns.

Breaking a pattern means changing your usual response. It takes effort and patience. Start by noticing when the pattern is happening. Write down what situation led to it and how you felt. Next, think about small changes you can try. If you always say yes to too many favors, practice saying no once a week. If you lose trust in people quickly, try to open up a little more slowly instead of shutting down. Breaking patterns is like training a muscle; it gets easier with practice.

Strengths You Didn't Know You Had Will Surface

Difficult experiences often show you strengths that you didn't realize were inside you. When things get tough, you may find you are braver, more patient, or more creative than you thought. For instance, someone who loses a job might discover they can learn new skills or start a project they always wanted to try. Hard times open the door to new parts of yourself.

To notice your strengths, look back at what you handled well during challenges. Maybe you stayed calm in a crisis or found ways to cheer yourself up. Write these down or share them with a friend. When you remind yourself of these abilities, it becomes easier to face future problems. Strengths grow when you use them with intention, like exercising a skill.

Values and Boundaries Become Clearer

Going through hard times often helps you understand what matters most to you. Values are the things you believe are important in life. Boundaries are limits you set to protect your well-being. For example, after feeling overwhelmed by too many commitments, you might realize that family time is a top value for you. Or after being hurt in a friendship, you might learn where you need to set boundaries about respect.

To find your values and boundaries, reflect on moments when you felt good and moments when you felt upset or drained. Ask yourself what was happening and why it mattered. Make a list of values like honesty, kindness, or independence. Then think about boundaries like saying no to extra work or choosing not to argue. Practice living according to these values and boundaries to keep yourself balanced.

Life is Not Random but a Series of Lessons

At first, life can feel like a mess of random events happening without reason. It is easy to feel lost or confused. But if you start to see life as a series of lessons, it changes your view. Every experience, especially the hard ones, can teach you something useful. This mindset makes the chaos easier to understand.

Try to take a moment each day or week to think about what you learned. For example, if you had a disagreement with a friend, think about what it showed you about communication or patience. If you made a mistake at work, consider what skills or knowledge you gained. Viewing life as lessons helps you realize that even setbacks and mistakes bring growth.

Detours, Disappointments, and Heartbreaks Shape You

Life does not always follow the path you expect. Sometimes you face detours where things don't go as planned. Disappointments happen when outcomes are not what you hoped for. Heartbreaks come from loss or sadness in relationships. These events can feel discouraging, but they also change who you are in important ways.

Think about a time when something didn't go your way, and how it affected you long term. Maybe you lost a chance for a job but found a better one later. Or a friendship ended, but it helped you become more independent. These experiences teach resilience, the ability to recover and keep going. They can also help you see what you truly want in life.

Meaning Transforms Pain into Insight

Meaning does not make pain go away, but it changes how you experience it. When you find meaning in a difficult time, you turn suffering into something more useful. Instead of just feeling hurt, you gain insight — a deeper understanding of yourself or life. For example, someone who struggles with illness might use that experience to help others or to appreciate good health more.

To find meaning, ask yourself how a challenge has changed you. What did you learn about your feelings, your values, and your strengths? Write your thoughts in a journal or talk to someone you trust. Meaning also comes from actions, like volunteering or teaching others what you learned. This process turns regret into wisdom, helping you grow even from painful moments.

Turn Lessons Into Your New Life Philosophy

Learning from Pain and Letting It Guide Your Life

When you go through tough times, it's normal to hurt or feel lost. But once you take the time to understand what happened and what you have learned from it, you can start to use those lessons to shape how you live your life. The experiences you survive become a new base for you—a sort of personal way of seeing the world that is built on what you've been through, how honest you are with yourself, and your ability to keep going even when things are hard.

Discovering What Truly Matters

For example, maybe your difficulties showed you that you care more about peace than trying to make everyone around you happy. People-pleasing can feel like an easy way to avoid conflict, but it often leads to feeling drained or like you're not being true to yourself. Learning to value peace means you focus on calm and balance in your life instead of constantly worrying about what others think. To practice this, you might start setting small boundaries, such as saying "no" when you feel overwhelmed or choosing not to join conversations that bring stress.

Understanding Endings as Part of the Journey

Another important lesson might be that the end of something doesn't always mean you've failed. When a relationship, job, or phase of life ends, it can feel like a loss or a sign that you didn't do well. However, learning that endings are a normal part of life can change your view. Instead of beating yourself up, you can begin to see endings as opportunities for new beginnings. This can mean reflecting on what the experience taught you and making a plan for the next step. For instance, after a job ends, you could list new skills you want to learn and start looking for work that fits your interests better.

Recognizing the Value of Slowing Down

Sometimes, life moves so fast that it's easy to think slowing down is a weakness or wasting time. But pain can teach you that slowing down is actually a smart choice. It gives you time to think, recover, and make better decisions. Slowing down might mean taking a short break during your workday to breathe deeply or setting aside a few minutes in the morning to plan your day calmly. This helps avoid rushing into things that might cause more stress. When you allow yourself to slow down, you are showing yourself kindness and wisdom.

Building a Framework for Life from Your Lessons

These insights you gain from pain aren't just feelings or thoughts; they form a framework for how you live each day. This framework affects many parts of your life, starting with the choices you make. For example, knowing that peace matters more than pleasing others might lead you to choose friends who respect your boundaries. If you understand endings aren't failures, you might take risks without fear, knowing it's okay if things don't always work out.

Your boundaries—the limits you set in relationships and work—also change. Learning from pain often means you start to protect your energy and time better. You might decide not to answer texts late at night or stop agreeing to last-minute plans that stress you out. These boundaries show respect for yourself and help others know what you need to feel safe and happy.

Learning from tough experiences also influences how you love yourself and others. When you see yourself as a person who has survived and grown, you can be kinder to yourself. This might mean speaking gently inwardly instead of harshly criticizing yourself when things go wrong. It also helps you be more patient and compassionate toward others because you understand everyone has challenges.

Using Your Scars as Sources of Strength

Your scars, whether physical or emotional, remind you of the battles you've faced. Instead of feeling ashamed or hiding them, you can carry them with pride as signs of your strength. Think about a scar on your skin—it tells a story of healing. In the same way, emotional scars tell a story about the struggles you overcame. Carrying your insights forward means holding onto the lessons you've learned, not the pain itself.

To do this, try writing down the lessons your past has taught you. Putting these on paper can make them feel real and help you remember that you are stronger now than before. You can also share your story with a trusted friend or a support group. Talking about your experience helps turn your past into a tool for growth.

Choosing the Meaning of Your Past

Remember that your past shaped who you are, but it doesn't control you. You have the power to choose what meaning your experiences will have in your life. This means you don't have to let painful memories define your future. Instead, you can decide that these memories will serve as reminders to keep going, to love yourself, and to live life with more honesty.

This choice can feel freeing. For example, if you had a hard time in school and thought you were a failure, you can change the story to one where you worked hard and learned resilience. You get to be the person who decides how to use your past—not the other way around. This mindset helps you take control of your life and make choices that reflect who you want to become.

Closing Reflection

Finding meaning in the mess is one of the most powerful acts of healing. It's how you turn chaos into clarity and pain into purpose.

Your past experiences — the heartbreaks, the losses, the mistakes — are not wasted. They are the lessons that built your awareness, compassion, and courage.

So ask yourself today:

- *What did this pain teach me about who I am?*

- *What values will I carry forward because of it?*

- *How can I live differently now that I know what I know?*

When you find meaning in the mess, you're no longer defined by what broke you — you're defined by how you rose, learned, and rebuilt. That is the quiet power of starting over.

Chapter 14

Design a Future That Feels Like You

W hen you decide to start over, it's tempting to rush into rebuilding — to fill the empty spaces, to replace what was lost, to prove you're "doing better now." But starting over isn't about reconstruction; it's about *creation*.

This is your opportunity to design a life that feels deeply, unmistakably *yours*. A life that aligns with your true values, reflects who you've become, and measures success by authenticity rather than external approval.

You've already lived a version of life that wasn't quite right. Now, you get to design one that fits — not perfectly, but honestly.

Align Your Goals With Your True Values

When Everything Changes, It's Time to Rethink Your Goals

Life can shift in unexpected ways, and when it does, it's common to hold on tight to old goals just because they feel familiar. These might be targets you aimed for in the past or ones that society told you to want. But when you find yourself starting over, it's a good idea to pause and think carefully. Are the goals you have truly yours, or are you following a path set by others or your past self? This moment of change is a chance to look inward and decide what really matters to you now.

Building Goals from Your Core Values

True alignment between your goals and your life comes when you build your objectives from the foundation of your values. Values are the deep principles or beliefs that guide you, often without you even realizing it. Instead of setting goals based on what others expect of you or what you think you should achieve, focus on what feels authentic and true to your own nature.

For example, if one of your values is kindness, your goals might involve helping others or creating a more supportive community around you. If growth is important to you, your goals could include learning new skills or pushing yourself out of your comfort zone. The key is to move from a place of authenticity rather than obligation.

Questions to Find What Really Matters

To get clear on your values, ask yourself simple but meaningful questions. One good question is, *"What do I genuinely care about now?"* This helps you distinguish your current passions from old interests that might no longer fit your life. Take time to think about what excites you these days or what topics you find yourself drawn to naturally. For example, you might have loved partying in your youth but now find joy in quiet outdoor activities or spending time with family.

Another important question is, *"What makes me feel most alive, connected, or at peace?"* Notice moments in your daily life when you feel truly yourself. Maybe it's during a creative project, a conversation with a close friend, or a walk in nature. These feelings bring clues about your deeper self and can guide you toward goals that resonate emotionally.

Finally, consider asking, *"What do I want my life to stand for?"* This is about the legacy you want to create or the impact you want to have on the world. For example, you might want to be remembered as a kind leader, an innovative thinker, or someone who helped others through tough times. Your goals then become stepping stones to building that kind of life.

Aligning Goals and Values Brings Natural Motivation

When your goals connect with your values, motivation tends to come more easily. Instead of forcing yourself to follow a plan that feels empty or tiring, you feel energized and inspired. Imagine trying to run a race without any interest in the prize; it would be hard to keep going. But if the race is meaningful, you run with purpose and joy.

This shift means you stop chasing things just to meet expectations or earn approval from others. Instead, you start creating your own path. Your goals become a way to express who you truly are, rather than trying to fit into someone else's mold.

Moving from Fear and Pressure to Purpose

Starting over can sometimes bring feelings of fear, guilt, or pressure. Maybe you worry what others will think if you change direction or fail to achieve certain milestones. These feelings can cloud your judgment and lead you to pick goals that aren't right for you.

To avoid this, let your values be the blueprint for your new beginning. This means using your inner beliefs as a guide, not outside demands or emotions that make you feel stuck. For instance, instead of setting a goal to earn more money because you think it's expected, focus on what makes you happy or fulfilled. If financial security is important because it helps you feel safe, your goal might be to build a budget or save steadily rather than chasing quick riches.

Taking Action: Steps to Align Your Goals with Your Values

Start by writing down your current goals. Then, next to each goal, note which value it connects with or whether it feels out of place. This process will help you see where your goals fit with your true self and where changes might be needed.

Next, think about small steps you can take to move closer to your values. For example, if kindness is a value, you might set a goal to volunteer once a month or practice daily acts of generosity. If creativity matters, you could schedule regular time for drawing, writing, or exploring new ideas. Breaking big goals into manageable actions makes the process less overwhelming.

It also helps to check in with yourself regularly. Every few weeks or months, ask those key questions about what you care about and how you feel. Your values and priorities can shift over time, and keeping track lets you adjust your goals naturally.

Embracing Your New Beginning

Starting fresh is a chance to build a life that fits you better. By understanding your core values and aligning your goals with them, you create a solid foundation. This foundation supports motivation, action, and a deeper sense of satisfaction.

When you focus on your values instead of outside pressures or old habits, you open the door to a more authentic and meaningful life. This way, your next steps come from purpose rather than fear or obligation. And that makes all the difference in how you experience your journey ahead.

Don't Rebuild the Same Life You Walked Away From

Understanding the Pull to Rebuild What Was Familiar

When you have gone through a loss, failure, or a big change in your life, it's natural to want things to go back to the way they were. You may feel this strong urge to rebuild what you once had because it feels safe and known. For example, if someone lost their job, they might want to find a similar job quickly, hoping that getting back to the old routine will solve everything. This feeling often comes from a desire for comfort. Familiar things don't require a lot of new effort or thought, so we tend to lean towards them after a hard experience.

You might think to yourself, "If I can just get back to where I was, everything will be okay." This thought is common and understandable. It can give you a sense of hope and control. But while this feeling is powerful, it's important to recognize that simply returning to an old way of living might not actually help you grow or feel better in the long run.

Accepting That Your Old Life No Longer Fits

The life you had before that hard time may not fit who you are anymore. When you move through challenges, you change. Your values, your needs, and your views on life might shift in ways you didn't expect. Think about it like this: if you try on a pair of shoes you wore years ago, and your feet have grown, those old shoes might feel tight or uncomfortable now. It's similar with your life. What worked well before might now feel confining or even wrong.

You might have learned new things about yourself during your tough experiences. Perhaps you realized you want different friendships, a new career path, or a better way to manage your time. These new parts of who you are mean your life has to adapt. This is something to celebrate, even if it feels scary or confusing at first. Growing means you are moving forward, even if it doesn't look like the past.

Why Trying to Rebuild the Past Can Hold You Back

Trying to go back can often feel like putting on old clothes that used to fit perfectly but now restrict your movement. They may look familiar, but they don't allow you to breathe freely. In other words, holding on to the past life might limit your ability to try new things or feel comfortable in who you have become.

For example, imagine someone who used to love a particular hobby but found that after a life change, it no longer brings joy. If they keep forcing themselves to do it just to feel normal, they might miss out on discovering new interests that really suit their current self. The old life, just like those tight clothes, can hold you back from moving forward and feeling free.

Asking the Right Questions to Build a New Life

Instead of trying to recreate what you had, it helps to ask yourself some important questions. These questions guide you toward figuring out what you truly need and want now. The first question could be: *What did my old life lack that my new one needs?* Think about the parts of your life before that didn't feel good or complete. Did you have enough time for yourself? Were your relationships supportive? Did you take care of your health?

You can write down these answers and use them as a checklist to make sure your new life includes what was missing. For instance, if your old life lacked time for exercise or relaxation, you can plan to add daily walks or meditation breaks. It helps to be specific about what you want to change.

Another helpful question is: *What kind of life would feel lighter, truer, more aligned now?* This invites you to imagine a life where you feel authentic and at ease. Picture simple daily scenes—what does a typical morning look like? Are you doing work that excites you, spending time with people who lift you up, or exploring places that inspire you?

Answering this question could lead you to try new routines or hobbies that better match your current interests. For example, if you used to feel stressed by a busy schedule, you might work on building a slower, more peaceful pace in your new life.

Finally, ask yourself: *If I weren't trying to prove anything to anyone, what would I build?* This is a powerful question because sometimes we hold onto parts of our old life to impress others or meet expectations. When this pressure is removed, it becomes clearer what you truly want. Maybe instead of a high-pressure job, you want to start a small business that makes you happy but doesn't bring stress. Or perhaps you want to focus on close friendships rather than large social circles.

Thinking about these questions can take time, and it might help to talk them over with a trusted friend or write your thoughts in a journal. Creating a space to explore your feelings openly is part of the process.

Starting Over as a Chance to Create Something New

Starting over isn't just about fixing what was broken; it's about taking everything you've learned from your experiences and using that wisdom to build a new life. It's like having the chance to design a house from scratch, where you can plan every room to fit your needs, rather than trying to remodel an old house that doesn't suit you anymore.

This new phase allows you to leave behind patterns that didn't work and try healthier ones. For example, if you struggled with saying no in your old life, now you can set clearer boundaries with kindness and confidence. Or if you learned that your well-being improves with better sleep or nutrition, you can focus on building habits that support that.

Designing your life based on wisdom means you pay attention to what your experiences taught you. You might remember moments when you felt most alive or at peace, then work to bring more of those into your everyday life. If your past was full of stress or feeling stuck, your new life can prioritize rest and movement.

Taking Small Steps to Build Your New Life

It's important to remember that rebuilding your life takes time. You don't have to have everything figured out at once. Start with small, manageable steps. For instance, if you want to change your social life, you might start by reaching out to one old friend or joining a group that shares your interests.

If you want to improve your health, start with a short daily walk or cooking one healthy meal a week. These small actions add up over time and help you move toward a life that feels good.

It also helps to keep checking in with yourself. Are the changes making you feel lighter and happier? Are you bringing more truth and freedom into your life? Adjust your plan as you learn more about what works and what doesn't. Building a life aligned with who you are now is a process, not a race.

Making Peace with Change

Change can be hard because it asks us to let go of what we knew and loved. But it also opens doors to new possibilities. When you accept that your old life no longer fits, you open yourself to something bigger and more real. This acceptance doesn't happen overnight, but it is a key part of moving forward.

Try reminding yourself when you feel unsure that it's okay to take time, to explore, and to make mistakes. Change means trying new things and learning what feels right. This attitude helps you build a new life that isn't just a copy of the past but something fresh and true.

Choose Joy and Authenticity as Your New Metrics for Success

Redefining Success on Your Own Terms

For much of our lives, success is often seen the same way. People tend to think of success as having big achievements, a good job title, a high income, or recognition from others. These things are common ways to mark success, but they mostly come from outside of us. When you decide to start over or take a new path, you get the chance to think about what success really means for you. Instead of following what others say, you can create your own idea of success based on what feels right inside.

Success does not have to be about how much you get done or how you compare to others. It can be about feeling joy and being true to yourself. Joy and authenticity can guide your decisions better than external markers. If you base your life on what honestly makes you happy and fits who you are, you will find a kind of success that feels deeper and more lasting.

Using Joy and Authenticity as Your Guide

To live with joy and authenticity means you pay attention to your true feelings and values. It means asking yourself each day if what you are doing feels right for you personally. For example, before starting a new project or making a decision, you can pause and think, *"Does this activity feel like the real me?"* This simple question helps you check if what you are about to do matches who you want to be.

Another useful question is, *"Does this bring me joy, peace, or a sense of purpose?"* Joy is not about feeling happy all the time but finding meaning even during hard moments. Peace can come from knowing you are following the right path instead of chasing things that stress you. Purpose means having a reason that matters to you, whether it's helping others, creating art, or learning new skills.

You should also ask, "*Am I living in line with my values?*" Values are the ideas that are most important to you, like kindness, honesty, family, or growth. Living in alignment with your values means your actions match what you truly believe in. For example, if honesty is important to you, then telling the truth and being open should be part of your daily life, even when it is not easy.

Understanding Joy Beyond Just Happiness

Joy is often confused with happiness. Happiness is usually seen as a feeling that comes and goes depending on what happens around us. For example, buying a new gadget or getting a compliment might make us happy for a short time. Joy, however, is deeper and lasts longer. It comes from doing what feels meaningful to you, even when it requires effort.

Choosing joy means making decisions that bring a sense of fulfillment, even if they are sometimes hard. For instance, you might decide to spend time learning a new skill that challenges you or to help someone in need, even if it means extra work or discomfort. These choices may not always bring immediate happiness, but they give a stronger feeling of joy because they matter to you.

Not everyone finds joy in the same activities. For one person, joy might come from spending quiet time in nature. For another, it might be creating music or writing stories. The important thing is to find what works for you. You can start by trying different activities and noticing how they make you feel over time.

Authenticity Means Being Real, Not Perfect

Authenticity can be misunderstood as needing to be perfect or flawless. In reality, being authentic means being true to who you are, including all the messy and imperfect parts. Life is not always neat and tidy, and pretending to be perfect only leads to stress and feeling fake.

Living authentically means accepting yourself as you are and showing that side to others. For example, you might admit when you make a mistake or share your true opinions, even if they differ from what others expect. This honesty builds real connections and makes you feel more comfortable in your own skin.

Sometimes being authentic also means making choices that are a bit different from what society or your family expects. It takes courage to do this, but it helps you live a life that feels honest and full. For example, choosing a career that you love but is not traditional in your culture is a form of authenticity.

Making Your Life Feel Like Home

When joy and authenticity are the main things you follow, life starts to feel more comfortable and right. It feels like home because you are living in a way that fits who you really are. Your life does not have to be perfect or free of problems to feel this way.

Imagine a home that has some clutter but feels warm and welcoming because the people in it are honest and happy to be themselves. That is the kind of life joy and authenticity create. Even on days when things are difficult, you feel peace because you know you are not living someone else's story—you are living your own.

This feeling can come from small everyday choices, like being honest with a friend about how you feel or spending time each day on something that truly interests you. Over time, these choices build a life that feels real and satisfying.

Practical Steps to Embrace Joy and Authenticity

To bring more joy and authenticity into your life, start by checking in with yourself each morning. Take a moment to ask the questions mentioned earlier: *"Does this feel like me?"* and *"Does this bring me joy or align with my values?"* Write down your answers in a journal to make these reflections clear.

Next, try to notice moments when you feel most alive and true to yourself. These moments can give clues about what brings you joy. For example, if you feel happy and peaceful while painting or talking to a friend, try to include those activities more in your routine.

Also, practice honesty in small ways. Share your real thoughts with someone you trust or admit when you are struggling. Authenticity grows with practice and helps build self-confidence.

Remember that living this way does not mean you will always feel good. It means accepting all parts of life and yourself—the joyful moments and the hard ones. By choosing joy and authenticity, your life becomes your own story, written your way.

Closing Reflection

Designing a future that feels like you is the most creative act you can undertake. It's not about rebuilding the old structure — it's about designing something new from the ground up, guided by your deepest truths.

Align your goals with what matters most. Leave behind the life that no longer fits. Define success by joy, authenticity, and peace, not by comparison or expectation.

You've survived the collapse of one version of your life. Now you have the freedom to build again — intentionally, beautifully, and truthfully.

Let this be your new mantra:
I am not rebuilding the past. I am designing a future that feels like me.

Epilogue

Trust the Process

S mall steps often feel awkward. You might catch yourself doubting the choices you make or wishing things were different overnight. The new habits you form can seem strange, like wearing shoes that don't quite fit yet. That discomfort is part of everything changing beneath your feet, and though unsettling, it's a sign you're moving.

Every tiny change—a new morning routine, a gentle shift in mindset, a moment of saying "no" where you used to say "yes"—might not feel like much at first. But these small moves create ripples far beyond what you see. They build momentum toward a life you haven't fully imagined yet, one that suits the person you are becoming even when you don't fully believe it now.

Trust doesn't mean you have all the answers. It means accepting the uncertainty, leaning into it, and knowing that the odd feelings during change are temporary. They mark the stretch between who you were yesterday and who you're growing into. And every time you adjust, you clarify what feels right and what doesn't. This trial and error is progress, not failure.

Walking through discomfort with patience and kindness toward yourself rewires how you approach life. It teaches you resilience not by avoiding hard moments but by meeting them with curiosity. These small, strange steps are the way your future self guides you forward—quiet but steady footprints toward a new landscape of hope and possibility.

The Beauty of Beginning Again

Starting over isn't a single, grand event — it's a quiet, continual rhythm that hums beneath every chapter of our lives. We shed what no longer serves us, sometimes by choice, sometimes by circumstance, and we step — hesitant but hopeful — into what's next. Reinvention isn't about erasing who we were. It's about carrying forward the essence of ourselves while letting the rest fall away, like leaves making room for spring.

The truth is, there's no final version of "you." Life will keep inviting you to evolve — through heartbreak and healing, through success and stillness, through the ordinary days that ask you to be brave in small ways. Each time, you'll begin again. And each time, you'll find that beginning isn't a sign of failure — it's proof of your resilience, your adaptability, your will to live fully.

As you close this book, don't wait for the perfect moment to start over. The next version of your life doesn't require a dramatic change, only a quiet decision: *to try again.*

May you remember that reinvention is not a destination, but a lifelong art — one you already know how to practice. Because every sunrise, every breath, every "*I'll try again tomorrow*" is helping you get get back up!

www.ingramcontent.com/pod-product-compliance
Lightning Source LLC
Chambersburg PA
CBHW021224130626
46554CB00004B/1363